Teaching Improv
The Essential Handbook

Your step-by-step guide to teaching short form improv.

Written by Mel Paradis

A Beat by Beat Book
www.bbpress.com

Table of Contents

Introduction	1
How to Use This Book	2
Lesson Activity Overview	5
Lessons	6
Lesson 1: Teamwork and Trust	7
Lesson 2: Make Associations	11
Lesson 3: Yes, and	15
Lesson 4: Listen	19
Lesson 5: Relate	23
Lesson 6: Be Honest	26
Lesson 7: Be in the Present	30
Lesson 8: Tell A Story (Part I)	34
Lesson 9: Tell a Story (Part II)	40
Lesson 10: Develop Relationships	43
Lesson 11: Two Person Scenes (Part I)	48
Lesson 12: Two Person Scenes (Part II)	52
Lesson 13: Group Scenes	56
Lesson 14: Guessing Games	60
Lesson 15: Practice for Performance & Creating a Line-Up	63
Lesson 16: Performance	67
Appendixes	69
Appendix A: Troubleshooting	70
Appendix B: Handouts	77
Appendix C: Lists	106
Appendix D: Sample Line-Ups	110
Appendix E: Final Performance Rubric	113
Appendix F: Additional Game Descriptions	114
Appendix G: Glossary of Terms	135
Appendix H: Bibliography, Resources, Acknowledgements	136

Teaching Improv: Bonus Digital Material (PDF Download)

- Printable versions of each homework assignment
- Links to every video referenced in this book

Download your copy for free at:
www.bbbpress.com/improv-bonus

Introduction

In recent years "improv" has become a buzzword in the world outside of theatre. Corporations and school districts have been adding improv workshops to their calendars at a rapid pace. Why? The skills needed to develop fabulous improv scenes are the same life skills that foster success in just about everything we do, including:

- *Teamwork*
- *Trust*
- *Agreement*
- *Adding to the discussion*
- *Listening*
- *Relating*
- *Being honest*
- *Being in the present moment*
- *Telling stories*
- *Developing relationships*
- *Making associations*

Whether you are a drama teacher looking to add a short form improv unit to your year, an improvisor wanting to lead workshops or a general education teacher looking for new ways to incorporate creativity, critical thinking, collaboration, and communication to your class, there is something in this book for you. I provide all the tools you need to empower your students with confidence through a sequence of skill-based lessons that can be easily integrated into any program.

While there are countless books and websites out there with improv games, many of them lack lesson-by-lesson strategies for teaching improv skills. The books that do teach skills are geared towards long form improv for adults. I wrote this book to save you the time of pouring through those books and websites. The lessons presented here are an amalgamation of years of research, teaching and performing.

Teaching Improv: The Essential Handbook is for both new and experienced improv teachers. This book was inspired by the format Denver Casado laid out in his first Beat by Beat Press book, *Teaching Drama: The Essential Handbook*. The lesson plans are written in a conversational, practical style to allow readers to feel like they are sitting in on one of my improv courses. Text written in italics represents how I would specifically communicate ideas and instructions. Once you get a feel for the "hows" and the "whys" of my teaching style, adapt it to your own.

However you decide to use this book, remember to follow the improv rules yourself as a teacher. A good improv class is like a scene. You never know what your students (scene partners) are going to bring to the table. If you are open to going with the flow and saying *yes, and* to the energy that your class brings, you will be rewarded with an amazing experience. And hopefully many laughs as well!

I got your back!

Mel

How to Use This Book

This book is divided into two parts; **Part One** contains the 16 step-by-step lesson plans that provide a comprehensive introduction to short form improv. **Part Two** contains the appendixes, a plethora of supplemental material to support each lesson. These appendixes include helpful lists for games and scenes, trouble-shooting tips, student hand-outs, grading rubrics, and much more. The appendixes are clearly referenced throughout each lesson so you can easily access them when teaching the course.

PART ONE: LESSONS

The lessons in *Teaching Improv: The Essential Handbook* are organized into three segments that build upon each other:

Lessons 1-10	Lessons 11-14	Lessons 15-16
Developing specific skills based on my 9 rules of improv, starting with the basic and building into the more complex.	Using those skills to create compelling and entertaining scenes and games.	Preparing scenes and games for a culminating performance.

The lessons can be condensed into a one day workshop or stretched out into an entire semester (or even year). Here are some suggestions for adapting them based on your program's needs:

General Education Teachers
A great way to run this program is to focus on each skill for approximately one month. Introduce the rule with the warm-up game and schedule in time throughout the month to play the remaining games in the lesson that reinforce that skill. Use the debrief time to connect the skill to your content area.

Drama/Improv Teachers
Focus on one skill for each session. Choose the activities that you feel will best resonate with your students. If you are limited in time, think about your objectives and look to the lesson overviews.

Workshop Facilitators
For a whole day workshop, break down the day into the nine rules and spend 30-40 minutes per rule, playing the games you find most compelling. If you are running a half day or evening workshop, I recommend limiting yourself to three rules. Teamwork, Yes, and and Tell a Story are good ones for an "Intro to Improv" program.

If you are new to teaching improv you can run the lessons as is, following them like a script. For those who have been teaching for years, use the lessons as a guideline and adapt as needed. The game debriefs include sample questions I would ask to reinforce the purpose of each activity. Try and get your students to come to these conclusions on their own whenever possible. I purposefully filled this book with obscure games and ones that I created to give even experienced teachers new ideas!

Each lesson includes optional games to substitute or extend your lesson. One asterisk (*) indicates a beginner game. Two asterisks (**) denotes an intermediate game. Three asterisks (***) is for advanced games.

Routines

Each lesson contains optional suggestions for homework and grading. Below are my recommended routines for those teachers using this book as a full curriculum.

Journals
Give each student a binder to use as a journal and to hold homework. Students should have a section for each rule/lesson where they can take notes on the rule, write summaries of games, house handouts and store graded homework.

Homework
Every lesson in the book includes a journal and a video reflection. Homework handouts are included in **Appendix B-1**. Printable versions of each of these handouts can be found in the "Bonus Digital Material" eBook that accompanies this paperback. Download it for free at www.bbbpress.com/improv-bonus.

Journal Reflection
The journal reflection is a way to assess if your students grasped the main ideas of the lesson. It is also used in later lessons to prep students for new games.

Video Reflection
It is essential that improvisors watch others improvise to improve their craft. This provides inspiration for how things can be done. The videos give students an opportunity to see a lesson in action and reflect on them. Later videos give students an opportunity to see games that will be played in the following lesson. I chose videos that were relatively short, clean (PG rated) and had good sound quality. You can find links to every video contained in this book in the "Bonus Digital Material" eBook that that accompanies this paperback. Download it for free at www.bbbpress.com/improv-bonus.

Grading

For those teachers who need to grade students, I have included a system of rubrics for class participation, homework and the final performance.

Class Participation Rubric

	3 Points	2 Points	1 Points	0 Point
RUBRIC	Was a respectful audience member AND participated actively in the lesson by adding to the discussion AND performing in scenes.	Was a respectful audience member AND participated in the lesson by adding to the discussion OR performing in the scenes.	Was a respectful audience member BUT did not participate in the lesson by adding to the discussion or performing in the scenes.	Was not a respectful audience member.

Homework Grade
Each lesson contains a specific rubric for the journal and video reflections. They are graded on a 0-3 point scale. 3 points if all parts of the assignment are completed. 1-2 points if they are missing items. 0 points if not completed at all.

Final Performance
The rubric for the final performance is located in *Appendix B: Handouts.*

PART TWO: APPENDIXES

The Appendixes are sections that I like to easily access when teaching improv. Keep them handy at all times. Here's an overview of each Appendix:

Appendix A: Troubleshooting
This is where you turn if you have a specific question about a problem you are having in your class.

Appendix B: Handouts
Printable homework sheets, scripts/handouts for specific lessons and a rubric and grading sheets for two-person scenes.

Appendix C: Lists
A comprehensive list of suggestions that you might need for a scene or game. If you are interested in a more random draw of locations, relationships or words, head over to http://www.can-i-get-a.com.

Appendix D: Sample Line-Ups
Ideas for planning out your class' final performance.

Appendix E: Final Performance Rubrics
A rubric for the final performance.

Appendix F: Glossary
A quick reference to all terms unique to improv. The first time these words are introduced in the book, they are highlighted in grey.

Appendix G: Additional Game Descriptions
You'll never run out of things to do in class with this bonus resource. Use these games as substitutes or extensions to lessons.

Appendix H: Bibliography and Resources
A list of books and websites that I have utilized over the years while compiling this curriculum. I also list a number of additional video links that demonstrate excellent improv skills.

Lesson Activity Overview

Lesson 1: Teamwork and Trust
Frisbee Whizzers
1,2,3,4,5
Body Hide
10 Second Object

Lesson 2: Make Associations
Duck, Duck, Cereal!
Da Doo Da Doo
Walk Over Association
Complementing Actions Game

Lesson 3: Yes, and
10% More
So I'll
Rumors
Create Obstacles

Lesson 4: Listen
30 Seconds of Character
Leaving the Couch
LECI
Two-Headed Interview

Lesson 5: Relate
Relating Circle
Mini-Armando

Lesson 6: Be Honest
Yes, Let's
Martha Game
I Believe
Martha Game Part II

Lesson 7: Be in the Present
Talking Heads
Surprise Movement
I'm Coming Over for Pancakes
Bump Set Spike

Lesson 8: Tell a Story (Part I)
Bad Stories
Ten Second Fairy Tale
Create a Conflict
Story Spine

Lesson 9: Tell a Story (Part II)
Five Word Group Story
String of Pearls
Slide Show
Bad Stories Part II

Lesson 10: Develop Relationships
We Both Want the Same Thing
High/Low Status Walk
10% More or Less Status
Status Switch

Lesson 11: Two Person Scenes (Part I)
Where Have My Fingers Been?
Good Script/Bad Script
Partner Scripted Scene

Lesson 12: Two Person Scenes (Part II)
Four Square
Sentences
New Choice

Lesson 13: Group Scenes
Alphabet Group Story
Old Job New Job
The Onion

Lesson 14: Guessing Games
What's My Job
Late for Class
Party Quirks

Lesson 15: Prepare for Performance and Creating a Line-Up

Lesson 16: Performance

Lessons

Lesson 1: Teamwork and Trust

> *"In the long history of humankind (and animal kind, too) those who learned to collaborate and improvise most effectively have prevailed."* -Charles Darwin

TEACHER OVERVIEW: Improv is a team sport. Students need to trust their fellow classmates in order to work well together. The games in this lesson help the class become comfortable with one another, which creates an environment for greater risks and creativity. This lesson also explores an introduction to improv and why it's important.

Teamwork: (verb) The process of working collaboratively with a group of people in order to achieve a goal

OBJECTIVE: Students will demonstrate an understanding of improv and begin to develop trust with their classmates.

Trust: (verb) to rely upon or place confidence in someone or something

MATERIALS:
- Journals for each student
- Homework handout for each student **(Appendix B-1)**

GREETING:
- As students arrive, greet them with a smile and have them join you in a circle.
- If you are new to the group, introduce yourself and play some name games (See Sidebar).
- *Today we are going to begin our journey into the world of improv. Let's start off with a silly warm-up game.*

WARM-UP: Frisbee Whizzers [Video in Bonus Digital Material]
- In this game, participants pass three phrases around the circle.
- The first is "Frisbee Whizzers," which always gets passed to the left. Beginning with the student to your left, pass the phrase all the way around the circle.
- The next phrase is "Misty Vistas," which always gets passed to the right. Beginning with the student to your right, pass the phrase "Misty Vistas" around the circle.
- Tell the students that you're going to begin a new round. They can choose either word, as long as they send it in the correct direction (Frisbee Whizzers = Left, Misty Vistas = Right)
- The third phrase, "Mr. Whiskers" is used to pass across the circle. Make strong eye contact with person you are passing to before saying the phrase.
- Continue the game using all three phrases - it's up to each individual student to decide which way to pass the phrase.
- Once they are comfortable, tell them that if a player says the wrong thing or laughs, they must take a lap around the circle and return to their spot. While they are gone, the game continues. If everyone becomes confused at any point, the whole class shuffles into a new spot in the circle, then resets and starts a new round.
- **Game Debrief:** *Did you feel silly playing this game? Did you laugh? In improv we must get out of our heads, not judge ourselves or others and be free to play. We must also always be aware of who has control of the "ball" or "focus" of the scene. Why did I emphasize eye contact when passing across*

Popular "Name Games" from the Beat by Beat blog:
- *Introductions & Applause*
- *Name Game*
- *Name Chant*

www.bbbpress.com/dramagames

Teaching Improv - A Beat by Beat Book

the circle? In improv we need to connect with the people we are playing with. Eye contact is the cornerstone of connecting.

DISCUSSION: What is Improv?
- With the class seated, explore:
- *What is improv? Has anyone ever seen an improv show? How is it different from other forms of acting?*
- Write responses on the board. Some points to hit on:
  - Acting without a script
  - Playing games where you get suggestions from other people
  - Scenes where you create everything as you go along
  - Sometimes serious, but most of the time associated with comedy
- *Over the course of the next several sessions we will explore improv, and the skills necessary to create great improv scenes. While there are several forms of improv (See Sidebar), in this class we will focus on short form. In short form improv, we get many suggestions from our audience and perform short scenes and games based on those suggestions. All our characters, stories and dialogue are created in real-time, in that moment.*
- *Improv works and doesn't turn into chaos because there are rules that the players follow. These rules help us create entertaining scenes for the audience. We will explore improv through these rules.*
- Write the 9 rules of improv on the board and briefly discuss each one. If possible, write the rules on chart paper so you can keep it handy for reference throughout the entire course:

Rules of Improv:

1. Teamwork and Trust
2. Make Associations
3. Yes…and
4. Listen
5. Relate
6. Be Honest
7. Be in the Present
8. Tell a Story
9. Develop Relationships

- *These rules apply far beyond improv performance. How might they help us in other parts of our lives (sports, scripted performances, relationships)? Discuss.*
- *Today we will focus on **Rule #1 Teamwork and Trust**. In order to perform on stage with a group (and work as a class), we need to work as a team, trust each other, and make our fellow performers look good. The activities today will help us begin to establish that trust and comfort.*

ACTIVITY: 1,2,3,4,5 *[Video in Bonus Digital Material]*
- Pair up students. If there is an uneven number, take a partner yourself.

History of Improv:
Improvisational theater dates back as early as Atellan Farce in the 300's BC in Ancient Rome. It later popped up in the 1500's in Europe as Commedia dell'Arte where bands of traveling performers would create shows with improvised dialogue. Modern improv as we know it came about in the early 20th century.

Forms of Improv:

Short Form: *Has roots in vaudeville. Acting exercises were developed by Viola Spolin in Chicago in the 1940's, and later continued by her son Paul Sills, who started The Second City. In the 1970's Keith Johnstone created the form of theater sports where players compete for audience or judge ratings. This form was popularized by the television show Whose Line Is It Anyway? and organizations such as ComedySportz. A short form show usually consists of several games (3-5 minutes long) with each game inspired by a different audience suggestion.*

Long Form: *Originally workshopped in San Francisco in the 1960's, it was solidified into a form by Del Close and Charna Halpern at the Improv Olympic (now iO) in Chicago. Currently the most famous theaters where long form improv is taught and performed in the US are The Groundlings, iO, Peoples Improv Theater and Upright Citizens Brigade. A long form show uses structure to interconnect several scenes, typically running 30 minutes, inspired by one suggestion.*

- Give each pair two minutes to learn three random, yet true facts about their partner.
- Gather everyone back into a circle. Each student will share those facts about their partner in a specific chant, that goes as follows:

ALL	STUDENT
1 (pause), 2, 3, 4, 5	My name is [Mel], and I say hi!
6 (pause), 7, 8, 9 10	This is [Bob] and he's my friend
1	He can ride a unicycle
2	He plays kazoo
3	He loves bubblegum ice cream
More, more, more, more!	
(Repeat with the next student in the circle)	

- **Game Debrief:** *What were some of the most interesting things we learned about our classmates? The more we know about our classmates, the more we can relate to them, and the more comfortable we will be with them on stage.*

ACTIVITY: Body Hide
- Ask for five volunteers to take the "stage."
- Explain the goal is for four of the students to use their bodies to hide the fifth student.
- The rest of the class' job is to try and spot any part of the hidden student's body, clothes or shoes.
- After playing a few rounds, consider shrinking the size of the groups to four, three, then two. (When working with smaller groups allow them to use walls for assistance).
- **Game Debrief:** *Were you comfortable or uncomfortable in this game? Did you trust that your partners were going to keep you safe? How did you communicate with each other? What worked best? Trust is crucial to successful improv. Often we get physical with each other on stage. It is important to be aware of our fellow improvisors and make sure they remain comfortable with those interactions. Communication facilitates trust.*

ACTIVITY: 10 Second Object
- Split up the class into groups of 4-6 students.
- Call out various objects. (Look to **Appendix C** for ideas).
- Groups have ten seconds to use their bodies to become that object.
- Example: Dog house: two or four students raise their hands to make the roof, one student makes an arch with their body as the front door, while another lays down inside as the dog.
- **Game Debrief:** *How did it go? Did anyone have trouble with multiple people trying to lead at the same time? In improv we must work together as a team to create. Sometimes this requires having a leader - allowing space for one person to take charge often keeps things from becoming chaotic. Just remember that no one person should always be the leader. Taking turns in that role is part of teamwork.*

WRAP-UP:
- *Today we focused on Rule #1: Teamwork and Trust. What helped facilitate teamwork and trust and why is it important to improv?*
- Pass out a journal to each student. *Throughout the course we will use a journal to keep notes.*
- *Let's start by labeling page one "Rules of Improv." Write down each of the nine rules.*
- *At the end of each lesson, label a new page with the rule of the day. Today's lesson is "Teamwork and Trust." Under Teamwork and Trust, write the names of the games we played. Next to each game,*

write a few words to summarize the game for future reference. We will do this every class. At the end of the course, we will review the games and decide which ones to play in our final performance.

HOMEWORK & RUBRIC:
- Your journal will also be used for two homework assignments after each lesson. One will be a short written assignment related to the rule of the day. The other will be a reflection about some video clips that you will watch online.
- These assignments will be graded on a 0-3 point Rubric. 3 points if you complete all aspects of the assignment, 1-2 points if you are missing elements and 0 points if it is not done. You will receive a hand out for each assignment with the expectations *(Appendix B-1)*.

Lesson 1: Journal Homework

Tonight your assignment is to write about a time when you needed teamwork to complete a task. How did things work out? Did the team work well together? What went well? If it didn't go smoothly, what went wrong? Did you trust the people in your group? Why or why not?

	3 Points	2 Points	1 Point	0 Points
RUBRIC	Student discussed a teamwork situation with details about how things turned out and a reflection of what went well or wrong.	Student discussed a teamwork situation but is missing details about how things turned out or is missing the reflection of what went well or wrong.	Student discussed a teamwork situation but is missing details about how things turned out AND is missing a reflection of what went well or wrong.	Assignment not done.

Lesson 1: Video Homework

Watch the video clips that are listed below. Write a short reflection about what these clips have in common. What scene or game was your favorite? Why?

Whose Line Is It Anyway? UK: Secret - Priests in a Church
https://youtu.be/fBfLFt8l038

Improv-A-Ganza: Sound Effects - Race Care Drivers
https://youtu.be/ek79sMX235k

Whose Line Is It Anyway: Hollywood Director - Convicts Escaping a Chain Gang
https://youtu.be/XCPBPXKakOQ

	3 Points	2 Points	1 Point	0 Points
RUBRIC	Student wrote a reflection including what the clips had in common AND listed their favorite game and why they liked it.	Student wrote a reflection including what the clips had in common OR listed their favorite game and why they liked it.	Student wrote a reflection, but it is missing what the clips had in common AND/OR student only listed their favorite game but not why they liked it.	Assignment not done.

ALTERNATE ACTIVITIES for this lesson *(Appendix G)*:
- Cross the Circle (Round One): This is another great "name game."
- Monty Python Tag*
- Enemy Protector*
- Great Machine*
- Bunny Bunny*

Lesson 2: Make Associations

> *"The strange thing is the brain connects things. Cat, bird, nest, tree, grass, house, sun, smoke. That's what the brain does. It doesn't go sausage, Mrs. Thatcher."* -Keith Johnstone, creator of Theatersports

TEACHER OVERVIEW: Making associations through words or actions helps improvisors create something based on a suggestion. For those students who think "I can't think of anything to say," these activities help open the gates of creativity.

Association: (noun) a mental connection between ideas or things

OBJECTIVE: Students will practice making associations and discover tools to help them think quickly and creatively.

MATERIALS:
- Homework handout for each student *(Appendix B-1)*

GREETING:
- Gather students in a standing circle.
- If homework was assigned, ask a few students to share their journal entries and reflect on the assigned videos. Lead into…
  - *Those improvisors have been working together for years. They trust each other and work seamlessly as a team.*
  - *As you probably noticed, they also came up with ideas very quickly. I'm sure some of you thought, "I can't do that. I couldn't think of anything to say!"*
  - *They created those scenes based on associations they made in their heads.*
  - *What were some associations you saw made in those videos?*
- *An association is a connection or a link between two things.*
- *Associations give us something to work with, that we can then build upon.*
- *Today we are going to practice creating words and actions based on associations.*

WARM UP: Duck, Duck, Cereal!
- *For our first activity, we're going to play a variation of Duck, Duck, Goose!*
- Remain in a standing circle. Explain the rules:
- This game is played like Duck Duck Goose, but instead of Goose, "It" tags a student and assigns them a category. Then "It" runs around the circle and tries to get back to the person they tagged before that student can name three things from the assigned category.
  - *Example: "Duck, duck, duck, cereal!"* "It" runs around the circle, while the tagged student says, "Cheerios, Frosted Flakes, Kix."
- If the student is able to say three things before "It" gets back to them, "It" continues walking around the circle and starts the round again. If the student from the circle does not come up with three things before "It" gets to them, they are now "It."
- **Game Debrief:** *How was it trying to come up with three things under pressure? We all have the capacity to quickly generate ideas, but it is something that comes easier with practice.*

DISCUSSION: Associations
- *As we discussed at the beginning of this lesson, using associations is one tool that improvisors have to come up with words or actions while on stage.*
- *In the last game we got a category and thought of three things from that category.*
- *Sometimes we just get a word and need to go with the first thing that comes to our mind in relation to that word. For instance, if I say "blue", you might say... (gesture for the students to call out random words). Were any of these associations wrong? Nope. Whatever comes to mind is perfectly acceptable. Let's practice...*

ACTIVITY: Da Do Da Do *[Video Link in Bonus Digital Material]*
- Remain in a standing circle.
- First, Student A says a word, such as *apple*.
- The student next to them, Student B, says the first word that pops into their head, such as *pear*.
- Everyone then says the two words together and finishes with the chant "Da Doo Da Doo"
  - Example: "Apple...Pear...Apple Pear, Da Doo Da Doo!"
- The game continues around the circle, this time with Student B providing the first word and the student next to them providing the associated word.
- If your students have rhythm, you can do this while snapping. *Apple...(snap)...pear...(snap)...apple pear (snap on pear) da do da doo (snap on second doo).*
- **Game Debrief:** *Did you notice some words end up completely unrelated? That's totally fine! Sometimes the first thing you think of is not associated at all with what was said before you. Our next game is going to explore this idea a little further...*

ACTIVITY: Walk Over Association
- Have the students stand in a horizontal line on one end of the stage facing the other end of the stage.
- Prompt the students with a random word suggestion.
- Students are allowed to take one step forward for each word they free associate with the suggestion.
- The goal is to get to the other side of the stage.
- Consider making it a race to see who can get to the other side first.
- *Example: Couch: big, comfy, red, lazy, movie, sleep, nap, etc.*
- For advanced students, consider providing two words - they must "associate" their way across the stage connecting the two words by the time they reach the other side.
- **Game Debrief:** *In improv, scenes move forward by making small associations, one step at a time. Sometimes you or your scene partner may say something that is unrelated to anything already created in the scene. This is a great time to use associations to get you from point A to point B.*

DISCUSSION: Actions as Associations
- *In improv we also create associations based on actions.*
- Write the following words on the board:

> ***Pantomime:*** *The act of communicating an action or an emotion without words.*
> ***Object Work:*** *The act of miming the use of non-existent objects.*
> ***Environment Work:*** *The act of creating the "where" in a scene through pantomime.*

ACTIVITY: Complementing Actions Game *[Video in Bonus Digital Material]*
- Start by discussing/demonstrating good pantomiming skills:
- *Excellent improvisors perform good object work, environment work and pantomiming.*

- Come up with several everyday actions and practice them together.
  - Example: Using a broom, washing windows, playing different sports, etc.
- The game starts with you, the instructor, performing an action, such as hitting a baseball.
- The student to your right, Student A, performs an action that complements your baseball hitting, such as jumping up and down as an excited fan.
- Once Student A starts jumping up and down, you can stop hitting the baseball.
- The student to Student A's right, Student B, picks an action that complements A's jumping up and down. Student B might play air guitar as a musician at a rock concert.
- The game continues around the circle.
- **Game Debrief:** *You don't need words to make associations. Where did we start? Where did we end up? This is how good improv is created. You take one suggestion and by making more and more associations you end up in a dramatically different place. Audiences love this.*

WRAP UP:
- *Today we played many games that helped us make associations. In the coming days we will use these associations to build stories and form full improv scenes.*
- *For instance, let's say you are in a scene on stage and your partner is pantomiming playing hop scotch.*
- *You can quickly make an association that hop scotch is a game usually played on playgrounds by kids. Another game is tetherball.*
- *You can then start miming as if you are playing tetherball. By miming the tetherball you buy yourself a few moments to make some more associations in your head.*
- *You might then make a quick association with these games and recess. Recess is far better than being in class.*
- *Now you have enough associations in your head to make the statement, "Mikey, I am not going back into math class. Mrs. Smith has it out for me."*
- *We now have a scene involving two kids talking about their teacher while at recess.*

Lesson 2: Journal Homework

For homework you will create five association chains. Grab a magazine or a book that contains a lot of pictures. Open up to a random page and write down the first object you see. Open to another page and write down the first object you see on that page. In 4-6 steps, make a chain of associations to connect the two objects. Give yourself no more that one minute to make your connection.

Example:
High chair + headphones: High chair, feeding a baby, baby screaming, trying to escape, putting on headphones.

RUBRIC	3 Points	2 Points	1 Point	0 Points
	Student wrote 5 association chains.	Student wrote 3-4 association chains.	Student wrote 1-2 association chains.	Assignment not done.

Teaching Improv - A Beat by Beat Book

Lesson 2: Video Homework

Tonight you will watch two video clips of the game Freeze. This game is all about making new associations based on players' physical positions. While watching the videos think about associations that you would make based on some of the positions the actors are in. List three things that you would have done if you were in either of those games of Freeze. For instance, in the first video, when Wayne, Brad and Jonathan are back to back to back, I thought about a conga line. In the second video, with the downward dog position that Jeff Davis was in, I thought of a dog house. Don't overthink it. Whatever comes to your mind, use it. There is no wrong.

Improv-A-Ganza: Freeze
https://youtu.be/DZZH3RMATQY

Improv-A-Ganza: Freeze
https://youtu.be/qj__tWwUuIA

RUBRIC	3 Points	2 Points	1 Point	0 Points
	Student listed three things they would have done.	Student listed two things they would have done.	Student listed one thing they would have done.	Assignment not done.

ALTERNATE ACTIVITIES for this lesson (*Appendix G*):
- 3 Some*
- Malapropism*
- Mime Whispers*
  - Freeze**
- Barney*
- Threesome*

Lesson 3: Yes, and

> *"Just say yes and you'll figure it out afterwards,"*
> -Tina Fey, The Second City and Saturday Night Live

TEACHER OVERVIEW: "Yes, and" is truly one of the cornerstones to improvisation. If we cannot accept what our scene partner has given us and further add to it, our scenes (or creative brainstorming sessions) will go nowhere. In this lesson, students will learn to accept an offer and add to it. They will also practice using the next logical step as a means to expand their offer.

OBJECTIVE: Students will demonstrate the ability to accept a statement or action that they are given and add something to it.

Yes (exclamation): asserting that something is true or correct

And (conjunction): used to introduce an additional comment or interjection

MATERIALS:
- Homework handout for each student *(Appendix B-1)*

GREETING:
- Gather students in a circle.
- If homework was assigned:
  - *Did anyone have any particularly interesting associations from last night's homework that they want to share?*
  - *Any thoughts about the Freeze videos?*
- *Today we move onto the most well known rule of improv… "Yes, and…"*
- *Put simply, this means that we accept what we are given from our scene partners and add to it.*
- *In this first game, we will be accepting and adding to a motion and a sound from the person next to us.*

WARM-UP: 10% More
- Remain in a standing circle.
- The teacher starts a small physical motion and sound.
- The person to their left accepts the small motion, repeats it AND magnifies it 10%.
- For instance, if the teacher starts with a small wave and a quiet "hey," the person to their right will make the wave a little larger and might say, "heeey." The next person makes the wave larger and extends out the "heeeeeey."
- This goes around the circle with the motion and sound getting bigger and bigger.
- After it goes around the circle once or twice, start a new sound and motion and pass it around the circle in the other direction.
- **Game Debrief:** *Did the progression feel natural? Was there a moment where it jumped more than 10%? Successful improv scenes move in small increments. You will lose your audience if you take too big of leaps.*

DISCUSSION: Yes, And…
- *In improv we take what was presented before us, say "yes" to it and then heighten it.*

Teaching Improv - A Beat by Beat Book

- *Heightening is adding information that raises the stakes in a scene and makes it more interesting.*
- *As things get heightened, it makes for better scenes and that is where the humor lies.*
- *If we negate what is said or presented to us, then our scene partner is not going to trust us AND the scene will go nowhere.*
- Turn to the student to your right and ask them to say the line "That is a beautiful dress you're wearing" to you.
- Once they say the line, reply: *"This isn't a dress. It's a baseball uniform."*
- Does this feel like a good way to start a scene? No. I just blocked, or denied their offer to me.
- How would you feel if you were in a scene and your partner blocked your offer? Let's try this again.
- Cue student to say the line "That's a beautiful dress you're wearing." Reply, *"Thanks, I think it is pretty too."*
- This is slightly better - I "Yes-ed" the statement, but did not AND it as well. The scene didn't go anywhere. Let's give this one more try…
- Cue student to say one more time "That's a beautiful dress you're wearing."
- Reply with *"Thanks it is going to look beautiful on my wedding day."*
- Now I "Yes, And"-ed - I have accepted the statement and jumped to a "logical" step. I associated a dress with a wedding. This scene is now a bride trying on wedding dresses.
- It is our goal to always accept what is offered, and then heighten it. This is what we'll be practicing today.

ACTIVITY: So I'll *[Video in Bonus Digital Material]*
- Pair up students.
- Give everyone in the class the same starting prompt, such as "It is a rainy day."
- Students take turns accepting the statement said by their partner, then adding "So I'll…" and taking the story to the next logical step
- Before adding to a statement, students repeat what their partner said.
- Example:
  - Student A: "It is a rainy day, <u>so I'll</u> pull out my umbrella."
  - Student B: "What you're saying is 'you'll pull out your umbrella,' <u>so I'll</u> open the door for you."
  - Student A: "What you're saying is 'you'll open the door for me,' <u>so I'll</u> go for a walk."
- Let this go for 3-4 minutes.
- **Game Debrief:**
  - Who wants to share where you ended up in your story?
  - Hopefully some will end up in bizarre places.

DISCUSSION:
- We all started in the same spot, yet we all ended up in very different places. This is the fun of improv and associations. However some students ended up in very crazy places. When things get too extreme, does this help or hinder improv?
- For example, if I had said: 'So what you're saying is, it's a rainy day so I'll jump on this rollercoaster.'
- Does this make logical sense? Sure it was kind of funny, but it came out of left field and won't serve us in the long run. (See Sidebar: The Quick Joke).
- It's great to land in unexpected places, but you must take logical steps to get there.
- For example, let's go back to our wedding dress scene.

The Quick Joke

Whenever you get the chance, remind students of the Teamwork rule and how it includes a "sub-rule"… "Don't try to be funny alone." If they go for the quick joke, they aren't working as a team. Humor comes out of working together to heighten an honest situation.

- I "Yes, and-ed" by saying it would look great on my wedding day. The humor in improv, though, often comes from taking a suggestion and going to a logical place that WASN'T expected.
- This isn't an easy thing to do and you have to practice quite a bit.
- Watch where I take this...
- Cue student to say statement, "That's a beautiful dress you're wearing."
- "Thanks. The lace is going to look amazing as we jump out of this plane to say 'I do!'"
- I took the dress, decided it was a wedding dress and then decided that some people get married while skydiving.
- Sure this doesn't happen all the time, but it does happen.
- I yes, and-ed the offer and created a unique scene.
- It is always best to stick to the next logical step if you are at a loss for an idea, but it can be fun to take things to a logical place that was not expected. Let's practice...

ACTIVITY: Rumors
- Have the students sit in a circle.
- Student A points to a student across the circle, Student B, and says to them, "Did you hear about..." (insert the name of a famous person, an object, or a place).
- Student B accepts the offer and creates a ridiculous rumor.
- Example:
  - Student A: "Did you hear about the President of the Student Council?"
  - Student B: "Yes, she was impeached after no one showed up for the Homecoming Parade that she planned."
- Student B picks a student across the circle, points to them and asks them about a new rumor.
- Example:
  - Student B: "Did you hear about chicken noodle soup?"
  - Student C: "Yes, I heard that everyone in the cafeteria got food poisoning from it."
- **Game Debrief:** *Was it easier to come up with an opening statement or the heightened reply? Why?*

ACTIVITY: Creating Obstacles *[Video in Bonus Digital Material]*
- Review pantomiming and creating environments/locations.
- It is important that environments are also "Yes, and-ed."
- If someone closes a door, the next player should not walk through the door, they should open it.
- Brainstorm a list of possible obstacles (doors, animals, fences to climb, things to jump over, etc).
- In this game, two students participate in a slow motion chase scene from an action film.
- Student A is "chased" by Student B.
- Student A creates obstacles through pantomime and Student B accepts those obstacles and bypasses them as well.
- In order for the audience to believe this chase scene, Student A should imagine they are "running" in a real environment that they know. (Imagine your neighborhood, a city block in your town, a local park, the hallways of the school, etc).
- Allow several pairs of students to have a turn.
- **Game Debrief:** *Was it easier to be the chaser or the one being chased? Did you know what obstacles your partner was "throwing" at you? How did you figure them out?*

WRAP-UP:
- Today we focused on the rule "Yes, and..."
- We learned to accept the offers we are given and add to them. When we further the scene in a logical way, we heighten the drama.

Lesson 3: Journal Homework

In creating obstacles, we had to imagine a specific environment. Tonight for homework, in your journal, write ten specific locations. For instance, not just a beach, but Point Dume State Beach. Not a park, but Ruby Carson Memorial Park. Label the top of the page LOCATIONS. We will use this list as inspiration in future classes.

RUBRIC	3 Points	2 Points	1 Point	0 Points
	Student wrote 10 detailed locations.	Student wrote a list, but it contained less than 10 locations OR the locations were not specific.	Student wrote a list containing less than 10 locations AND the locations were not specific.	Assignment not done.

Lesson 3: Video Homework

Watch the Mick Napier You Tube Video Entitled "A Place of Yes." Watch how a scene works with acceptance and how it goes nowhere when there is negation. Then write a short reflection about what you thought of the video and the two performances.

Mick Napier: A Place of Yes
https://youtu.be/mYv4vAnnuts

RUBRIC	3 Points	2 Points	1 Point	0 Points
	Student wrote a reflection that included specific references to both performances in the video.	Student wrote a reflection that included specific references to one of the performances in the video.	Student wrote a reflection but did not mention any specifics from the video.	Assignment not done.

ALTERNATE ACTIVITIES for this lesson *(Appendix G)*:
- Yes, and*
- Luckily Unluckily*
- Translate Gibberish*
- Yes Let's*
- Group Environment*
- Madison Avenue**
- Goalie**

Lesson 4: Listen

> *"People always go, 'I can't think that fast.' No, no, no, no. Don't think that fast. Just listen to the last thing he said."* -Keegan-Michael Key, The Second City and Key and Peele

TEACHER OVERVIEW: Listening is an integral skill to learn when working in any team. When doing scene work it is essential that you listen to what is presented and take it in before responding. You cannot "Yes, and" your scene partner if you don't know what they created, via words, actions or emotions.

Listen (verb): to pay attention to someone or something in order to hear what is being said

OBJECTIVE: Students will listen to each other by observing how their classmates move and absorbing what their classmates say.

MATERIALS:
- Timer
- Homework handout for each student *(Appendix B-1)*

GREETING:
- If homework was assigned:
  - *Does anyone want to share any thoughts on the Mick Napier video from your homework?*
  - *In the first scene, the actors in the video were listening to each other rather than just thinking of what they were going to say next.*
- *Today we are going to focus on the skill of listening.*
- *In order to listen, we need to focus on what our scene partner is really saying.*
- *Let's warm-up those listening skills.*

WARM-UP: 30 Seconds of Character
- Gather the class in a circle.
- Have everyone pick a character with a distinct voice in their head.
- This could be a southern belle, Forest Gump, a valley girl, Arnold Schwarzenegger, a New York cop, etc. (Look to **Appendix C** for more examples).
- It's OK for multiple students to play the same character.
- Tell the students to then pick a creature of fantasy, such as a dragon or unicorn.
- Give the class 30 seconds where they all simultaneously, in character, give a monologue about the creature.
- Example:
  - (spoken in an Arnold Schwarzenegger voice) *Unicorns are the most magical creature in all of the world. In fact I know that they are not imaginary. I have a pet unicorn that I keep in my bedroom. When I get home from school we go on a bike ride. The unicorn runs in front. If it is dark out, I put a light on his horn and it helps me stay safe...*
- *How did that go? Was it hard to stay focused? Were you able to stay in character? If not, why not? If we try to talk over our scene partners or conversely, if our scene partner never stops yapping, we can't listen.*
- Try the warm-up again, but this time going around the circle so that only one person speaks at a time.

Teaching Improv - A Beat by Beat Book

- Each student should allow the speaker about 30 seconds of monologue. At this time, the new student begins to speak and the previous student should stop and listen. Encourage students to feed off the same energy of the previous speaker.

DISCUSSION:
- *When you listen, you need to not only hear what your scene partner says, but watch them and feel their energy.*
- *This helps us connect and work in sync.*
- *When improvisors are in sync with each other, something called the Group Mind happens. When the Group Mind occurs, everyone on stage seems to be working as one. (See Sidebar).*

> **Group Mind:**
>
> *This phenomena occurs when a group is listening and relating to each other so well that they seem to work as one. Their movements may be in conjunction (as in the game Leaving the Couch) or their ideas are so in sync that the creation of a scene appears seamless.*

ACTIVITY: Leaving the Couch *[Video in Bonus Digital Material]*
- Ask 4 students to take the stage and sit on a "couch" (4 chairs next to each other).
- Students may not talk with one another in this game.
- One student takes focus and starts doing a simple repetitive motion, such as scratching their knee or sighing while leaning their head back.
- Other students join in with the motion.
- Once everyone is doing the same thing they should start "10% more"ing the action until they come to a climax.
- Students need to listen and watch each other to determine when they can no longer 10% more the base action.
- When they reach the climax, everyone stands at the same moment and leaves the couch. Start again with 4 new players.
- If needed, direct the group to slowly crescendo their moves and remind them when they are all at the highest point. Each subsequent group will get better and better at standing in unison.
- **Game Debrief:** *How did this game involve listening? If you were on the end of the couch did you know what was going on at the other end? Who took the lead? Why did you take the lead? How did you know that it was time to stand up? Did you trust the group?*

DISCUSSION:
- *Sometimes, as in the last game, we need to listen to and feel the energy of the group in order to move forward with a scene.*
- *Watching and listening for minute details helps us pick up on subtle clues as to what our scene partner is trying to communicate with us.*

ACTIVITY: LECI (Location, Emotion, Career, Injury)
- This is similar to the game telephone; one student gets information that they relay to another who in turn must relay to a final student who guesses what the original information was.
- Ask 3 students to take the stage, Students A, B and C. Ask Students B and C to leave the room.
- While they are gone, the group decides on a:
  - 1) Location (i.e. Coffee Shop)
  - 2) Emotion + Career (i.e. giddy Brain Surgeon)
  - 3) Injury (i.e. broke leg while skiing)
- Student B returns to the room. Student A gets three minutes to pantomime and/or speak in gibberish to communicate the location, emotional career and injury.
- Then, Student C enters and Student B must communicate the LECI to Student C.

- It is Student B's job to listen with their eyes and ears so that they can convey the items to Student C when they enter the room.
- Even if Student B does not know what they are pantomiming, they should try and approximate Student A's performance as best as they can.
- Once Student B spends three minutes, Student C guesses what they were.
- Send another two players out of the room and start another round.
- **Game Debrief:** *How do you think you did as a communicator in this game? Part of our job as improvisors is being strong communicators. If we are not clear, or give off bad signals (i.e. portraying our emotion as happy when in fact we are sad) we confuse others. What tricks did you use to listen and remember?*

ACTIVITY: Two-Headed Interview
- Ask four students to take the stage. Partner them up, Partners A and Partners B.
- These partners will be giving an interview as a "two-headed" people.
  - Partners A speak one word at a time. One person says a word and the other person adds the next word to the sentence, etc.
  - Partners B speak simultaneously. The partners must watch each others' lips to say the same words together.
- Get a suggestion from the class of an expertise.
- The class asks questions about that topic for the two-headed people to answer. Try and avoid simple yes or no questions.
  - Example: Experts on making ice cream. Question from the class: "How do you decide what flavor of ice cream to make?"
    - Partners A (Alternating one word at a time): *"We" "think" "that" "every" "day" "a" "new" "flavor" "should" "be" "made." "We" "choose" "the" "flavor" "by" "looking" "out" "the" "window" "and" "seeing" "what" "is" "there."*
    - Partners B (speaking simultaneously): *"Weeeee llliiike tooooo loooook iiiin ouuuur rrrrreeeeeefrigerator to seeee wwwwhaat fooooood iiiis thhhhere."*
- Each round may go for a few questions then give new students a chance to play. Both sets of partners must listen but they will be listening in different ways:
  - <u>One Word at a Time</u>: Avoid too many "ands" and "because" or the answer will lose focus.
  - <u>Speaking Simultaneously</u>: One person should be the leader and the other follows. Make sure you change up the leadership.
- **Game Debrief:** *Was it easier to speak simultaneously or one word at a time? Why? How did you listen to your partner? How did you decide who would take the lead and who would follow?*

WRAP-UP:
- *Today we focused on listening. If we do not listen, we cannot "Yes, and" our classmates.*
- *Whether you realized it or not, by listening to your fellow classmates, you build their trust and form a stronger team.*
- *Strong teams are capable of creating a Group Mind that makes audiences feel like entertaining improv scenes are being created effortlessly.*

Lesson 4: Journal Homework

In the warm-up we used stock characters with unique voices. For tonights homework you must come up with a list of ten different characters that an actor could use in a scene. They may be basic characters, such as a doctor or teacher or very specific characters, such as Wonder Woman or a pirate who has lost their treasure. You can use any of these characters in future classes when you need to endow another performer with a character ("You are an angry preschooler") or whenever you want to become a specific character in a scene.

RUBRIC	3 Points	2 Points	1 Point	0 Points
	Student wrote a list of 10 characters.	Student wrote a list of 5-9 characters.	Student wrote a list of 1-4 characters.	Assignment not done.

Lesson 4: Video Homework

Watch the following videos from Canadian Improv Games and One Minute Improv on listening. These videos sum up what we talked about today and give a little added information about how listening can help you in a scene. Then watch the game Two-Headed Expert from Improv-A-Ganza. This is an example of how the two-headed people work together in an actual scene. List three times you noticed the players listening to one another.

Canadian Improv Games: Listening
http://improv.ca/listening/

One Minute Improv: Listening
https://youtu.be/b-31atJrKdI

Improv-A-Ganza: Two Headed Expert (Organic Chemistry)
https://youtu.be/y7YS8JbbqyQ

RUBRIC	3 Points	2 Points	1 Point	0 Points
	Student wrote three examples of listening.	Student wrote two examples of listening.	Student wrote one example of listening.	Assignment not done.

ALTERNATE GAMES for this Lesson *(Appendix G)*:
- Cross the Circle*
- Group Environment*
- Zen Counting*
- The Oracle*
- Pass the Clap with Words*
- Forward Reverse***

Lesson 5: Relate

> *"So, what is it? What's relating?...It's being so aware of the other person that, even if you have your back to them, you're observing them. It's letting everything about them affect you; not just their words, but also their tone of voice, their body language, even subtle things like where they're standing in the room or how they occupy a chair. Relating is letting all that seep into you and have an effect on how you respond to the other person."*
> -Alan Alda If I Understood You, Would I Have This Look on My Face?

OVERVIEW: In the previous lesson, students were introduced to the idea of listening. Today we take it one step further. Relating is listening, internalizing and connecting with whatever has been communicated.

OBJECTIVE: Students will listen and relate to their fellow classmates.

Relate (verb): to make or show a connection between; to feel sympathy for or identify with

GREETING:
- If homework was assigned:
  - Does anyone have anything they want to share about the videos you watched?
- *Before we get into the meat of our next lesson, let's get our bodies ready to listen and retain information.*
- Homework handout for each student *(Appendix B-1)*

WAMRUP: Relating Circle
- Have the class stand in a circle.
- Stand in the middle and make a strong character statement.
- The students think of characters who would be related to your character.
- As students come up with ideas they should step forward, in character, and deliver a response. Novice students should state who they are before delivering their line. Advanced students do not need to do this step.
  - Example: Teacher Statement: *I was nominated for Prom King.*
    - Possible student reactions:
      - The Girlfriend: *Babe I am so excited for you!*
      - A student who wasn't nominated: *Oh, good for you, Mike* (said through gritted teeth).
      - Guidance Counselor: *College Application Boards do not care if you were Prom King. You need to take an SAT prep course, Mike.*
- Continue for a few rounds.

Using Names:
Note the use of names (Babe, Mike) in the strong statements made in the game Relating Circle. When we endow actors with names and then use them throughout a scene, it helps develop relationships and makes those relationships relatable for the audience.

DISCUSSION:
- *We often forget that listening does not just involve hearing what someone says, but taking it in and holding onto it for as long as needed so that we can respond.*
- *These responses include the expressions we relay on our faces and with our body posture.*
- *If someone tells you that they ate caramel corn, got on a roller coast at the county fair and then vomited all over their girlfriend, your face may cringe or you might burst out laughing.*
- *It all depends on how you relate to the person telling the story.*

Teaching Improv - A Beat by Beat Book

- *If you are the storyteller's mother, you might cringe. This is your child. You want the best for them. You know that this experience was likely embarrassing. You might give kind words of sympathy.*
- *If you are the storyteller's best friend, you might laugh. Perhaps you don't like the girlfriend because she is getting in the way of your friendship. Your response might be to make fun of your friend.*
- *In improv we get to step into the shoes of characters outside of ourselves and react in scenes as those characters.*
- *It is essential that we connect and relate to our characters so that our responses to the situations and the dialogue are genuine.*
- *Today we are going to practice this using a popular structure in improv called the Armando.*

ACTIVITY: Mini-Armando
- Ask 6-8 students to form a back line on the stage.
- Get a suggestion from the audience of a "first time in life event" (i.e. first sleep over, first lost tooth, etc).
- As the teacher, you will improvise a monologue about your life based on that suggestion. If the suggestion is "broken bone," tell the story of the first time that you broke a bone. (If you need to, fabricate a story or make up details, but play it off as something that actually happened).
- Tell what happened before the event, during the event and after the event. Try and include a couple of other characters in each part and give as many details as you can.
- The students step forward to recreate the *before, during* and *after* in three separate improvised scenes.
- Notes:
  - The teacher edits the three scenes with a clap or ring of the bell to keep the story moving along. (For more on editing see the Sidebar on p 30).
  - Not all students will be in each scene.
  - Students should remain the same characters in each scene.
  - If there are not enough characters for each student to play, encourage students to become pieces of the environment. (i.e. If the bone was broken while riding a horse in the woods, one student becomes the horse, others become trees).
- Encourage students to listen carefully to the details of your monologue.
- Students need to relate to the story so that they can express proper emotions and create dialogue.
- They also need to relate to the other performers on stage so that the dialogue is genuine.
- Tell the students that one tip for making the scenes more interesting is for the players to have an opinion about the story. This will help them remember details, give them something to relate to and something to play up.
  - For example, if it's their opinion that you were at fault for falling off the horse, they might play you as an idiot in the scene. If they think the wrangler was unsympathetic to your injury, they should play them as such.
- When students are finished with their three scenes, choose 6-8 new students to take the back line and get a suggestions for a new "first."
- **Game Debrief:** *Were you able to relate to my monologues? Was it easy or difficult to create the scenes and characters? Did it help to form an opinion?*

> **The Armando:**
> The Armando is a long form improv format created by Armando Diaz and other Chicago improvisors. In a true Armando, the audience provides a suggestion. A monologist steps forward and tells a true story based on that suggestion. Improvisors listen to the story, relate to the monologist and perform a series of 3-4 scenes based off of things they gleaned from the monologue. The monologist then steps forward again, giving another monologue based on something from one of the scenes. Improvisors perform 3-4 more scenes. There is one more monologue to end the game. Armandos typically last 15-30 minutes.

WRAP-UP:
- *Listening and relating go hand in hand.*
- *Listening allows us to "Yes" our scene partner.*
- *But if we only listen enough to be able to come up with our next line of dialogue, those responses will be flat.*
- *When we also relate to what they are saying, we step into the character and make associations and assumptions based on that character.*
- *We are now able to "and" the offer. This is what makes for enjoyable improv.*

Lesson 5: Video Homework

Tonight I want you to start with the video portion of your homework. Watch the following video of The Laff Staff performing an Armando on stage. In a typical Armando, players do not perform the stories literally, as we did in class (with the beginning, middle and end), but instead take ideas they get from relating to the story told. These ideas are turned into scenes "based" off the monologue. Name three "items" picked out from one of the monologues that were brought into the performance. These could be an emotion, a character, a location, an idea, etc.

The Laff Staff: Armando
https://youtu.be/bPqX4H3qGFw

RUBRIC	3 Points	2 Points	1 Point	0 Points
	Student wrote three items gleaned from one of the monologues.	Student wrote two items gleaned from one of the monologues.	Student wrote one item gleaned from one of the monologues.	Assignment not done.

Lesson 5: Journal Homework

Tonight for homework, I want you to go to http://www.can-i-get-a.com. Click on the location, relationship, or word button. This is going to be your suggestion. Use that word to spark a memory from your life. If you can't come up with anything, click another button until you find something that gives you an idea. Write the story in your journal. Make sure you fill in lots of details. If we were doing an Armando, this would be your "monologue."

RUBRIC	3 Points	2 Points	1 Point	0 Points
	Student wrote a detailed story based on a suggestion.	Student wrote a basic story based on the suggestion.	Student wrote ideas, but they were not connected into a story.	Assignment not done.

ALTERNATE GAMES for this lesson:
- Silent Scenes*
- I Believe*

Lesson 6: Be Honest

> *"Finding honesty is a deceptively simple endeavor that involves as much not doing (not panicking, not bluffing, not doubting) as doing (being present, listening, paying attention)."*
> -TJ Jagodowski and Dave Pasquesi, Improvisation at the Speed of Life

OVERVIEW: Honesty in improv is an essential ingredient to creating believable, entertaining scenes. When actors play their environments, objects and characters honestly, the audience is more likely to go along for the ride.

OBJECTIVE: Students will demonstrate honesty in their creation of environments, objects and characters.

Honesty: (noun) the quality of being true and sincere; free from deceit or fraud

MATERIALS:
- Homework handout for each student *(Appendix B-1)*

GREETING:
- *If homework was assigned:*
  - *What did you think of the Armando from the video homework?*
  - *Did you believe the improvisors were the characters they were portraying? Why?*
- *Today we are going to explore honesty in improv.*
- *We will look at it from the perspectives of:*
  1) *working with objects*
  2) *interacting with environments*
  3) *portraying characters*
- *Let's begin with an "object work" exercise.*

WARM UP: Yes, Let's
- Have students spread out throughout the room.
- When you call a student's name, they say "Let's (do a specific activity)."
- The class accepts the activity by saying, "Yes, let's."
- Everyone pantomimes the activity.
  - Example: "Let's dig a hole to China." Class: "Yes, let's!" (Everyone pantomimes digging a hole). "Let's catch loose chickens in the yard." Class: "Yes, let's." (Students run around the room chasing chickens).
- **Game Debrief:** *How physically honest were you with the activities you were engaged in? Could you see and feel the objects in your hands?*

DISCUSSION:
- *Honesty in improvisation means playing things as real as possible.*
- *An improvisor must see and feel the objects that they are working with in order for the audience to buy into the reality of what is being created on stage.*
- *In addition to working with objects, we want the audience to believe we are where we say we are.*
- *We want them to watch us walking around the state fair and "smell" the cotton candy or "see" the ring flying from our hand in the ring toss game.*

- *A trick that most improvisors use at some point or another is to become a piece of the environment in a scene, rather than a character.*
- *This is all part of give and take.*
- *Sometimes you take the lead character and other times you become part of the set and support the lead characters. In this next game we will use associations to come up with honest objects and characters found in variety of environments.*

ACTIVITY: Martha Game
- Get a suggestion for a location or use one from **Appendix C**.
- Four students enter the stage one at a time announcing they are an object found in that environment.
- The fifth student comes out and plays a character found in that environment.
  - Example: *Beach*
  - First student enters and says, "I am a beach chair" and lays down like a beach chair.
  - Next student enters and says, "I am an umbrella" and becomes an umbrella.
  - Third and fourth students become a wave lapping up the beach and a sea gull eating trash.
  - The fifth student enters as an ice cream vendor. Clear the stage, with the phrase "Scene!" (See Sidebar on Editing)
- Run several more rounds with different locations.
- **Game Debrief:** *How did we do as a class creating honest environments? Did anything stick out or distract from the environment?*

DISCUSSION:
- If we have honest environments and our object work is good, but our characters are not believable, we lose our audiences' trust.
- An important component of playing honest characters is playing honest emotions.

ACTIVITY: I Believe *[Video in Bonus Digital Material]*
- Have the class stand in a circle.
- Round One: Each student takes a turn stepping forward and shares a random but true fact about themselves.
  - Example: "I love spicy food."
- Round Two: Students take turns stepping forward to share something they believe in. This can be silly or serious, but it must be true.
  - Example: "I believe raw sea urchin is the most disgusting food in the world."
- Round Three: Students think about something they DON'T believe in, but then step forward as a character who DOES believe in that thing.
  - Example: "I believe in giving everyone who participates in a sport a trophy at the end of the season. In fact, I think this year we need to make plaques, not just for 1st place, 2nd place and 3rd place teams, but for every kid who played in little league. Sure, some kids spent every

---

Editing

To edit a scene is to interrupt or end it. Learning how and when to do this takes time and practice. Ending a scene can be done through:
- *a blackout*
- *an off-stage person calling "Scene!"*
- *a clap-out: a player on the back line claps their hands*
- *a "sweep": a player steps from the back line and walks across the stage in front of the actors to indicate that their scene is over. The player who sweeps usually initiates a new scene. (This is done in mid and long form games that are comprised of several scenes based off one suggestion).*

The best editing happens when improvisors have had enough time to set up their premise, play with that premise and reach a high point with a good laugh.

NOTE: Consider having the students write these "opposite" characters down for use in future scenes.

game picking flowers on the field and their teams lost, but those kids need to know that they are elite athletes too! Maybe if they get a trophy it will encourage them to play harder next season."
- **Game Debrief:** *Sometimes in improv you'll be required to play a character opposite of your intuition. It's important to be able to relate to these characters and play them honestly.*

DISCUSSION:
- Let's continue to explore this…
- Playing honest opposites is also a great way to add nuance and humor to our improv scenes.
- If a group sets up a scene that is grounded in honesty, with everyone playing their parts sincerely, one person can play opposite of preconceived truth.
- Back to the beach example. There was the chair, umbrella, waves, a sea gull and an ice cream vendor. A sixth student could enter the scene as a hot chocolate vendor. That student is playing opposite of what is expected and desired at a beach. Who wants hot cocoa? If this were a scene, the conflict could be the two vendors vying for more customers. The game within the game (See Sidebar) could be that the hot chocolate vendor is more successful than the ice cream vendor. Additional players could walk on, buy hot chocolate and walk off. (A walk on is when a player who has not been part of a scene, walks on, briefly adds to the scene through short dialogue or a motion, and then exits the stage. We will cover this more when we do our lesson on group scenes). The hot chocolate vendor could even heighten their position by continuing to offer more and more ridiculous cold weather items, such as scarves, mittens, hats, coats and heaters.
- Let's practice this…

> **The Game Within the Game**
>
> *Some of the best improv comes from performers Playing the Game Within the Game. The game is any pattern that evolves within a scene. Performers play it by continuing the pattern and heightening it. As students of improv learn the basics it is worthwhile to explore this concept. Like all the rest of the "rules," when it is absorbed and in their back of your head, it makes performing improv more enjoyable.*

ACTIVITY: Martha Game Part II
- Have the class stand in a horseshoe facing downstage.
- Six students take turns stepping forward to join an "environment":
  - The first four students to step forward enter as objects found in the environment.
  - The fifth student announces themself as a character found in the environment.
  - The sixth student enters as a character that is *opposite* of what would be expected in the environment.
- Allow this to turn into a full scene or edit after the sixth student steps forward.
- The following are examples to get creativity flowing:
  - <u>Beach</u>: sandcastle, cooler, pelican, dead fish, sunbather, lifeguard who can't swim
  - <u>Library</u>: bookshelf, table, computer, fish tank, student engrossed in their book, librarian who yells instead of whispering
  - <u>Doctor's Office</u>: examining table, stethoscope, container of tongue depressors, health chart, patient in for a wellness check up, nurse who is very unsanitary (sneezing, handing dirty tissues to patient)
  - <u>Haunted House</u>: spider web, creaky staircase, zombie, terrified child, really bored and not scary ghost
- **Game Debrief:** *Did we create honest environments? Was it easier to create a character we would find in that location or create the opposite type of character? What was it like when the opposite person entered the scene?*

WRAP-UP:
- *As we create our environments and characters we want to play them as honestly as possible.*
- *Remember that honesty in improv is a foundation to our scene work.*
- *Only through the lens of honesty can we play off opposites to find humor.*

Lesson 6: Journal Homework

In your journal create a character who is opposite from yourself. Draw a picture of what this character looks like. Give them a name, an age, an occupation, a family. Make it as detailed as possible (things they like, things they dislike). Make sure this is a character that you will be able to play, as we will be using these characters later in the class.

RUBRIC	3 Points	2 Points	1 Point	0 Points
	Student created a character, drew a picture of them and gave them a full backstory.	Student created a character with a basic backstory.	Student created a character without a backstory.	Assignment not done.

Lesson 6: Video Homework

Watch the following video clips and take note of the object and environment work. The first shows improvisors performing bad object work with actual props. Make a list of five mistakes to avoid with object work. The second video is a two person scene that includes good object, environment and character work. Finally, the last video is one scene from a long-form Armando where an improvisor goes through a very elaborate set of entries to get to a bomb shelter. He commits to his environment work and the audiences love it.

Chris Besler: How to Spot an Improvisor (Safe for Work Version)
https://youtu.be/3b1ZJBgJ5LM

Improv-A-Ganza: New Choice - Nice Restaurant
https://youtu.be/DxdLiE6Eq7E

iO: The Armando Diaz Show - Jason Entry
https://youtu.be/kr5xjoOnAec

RUBRIC	3 Points	2 Points	1 Point	0 Points
	Student wrote 5 mistakes to avoid.	Student wrote 3-4 mistakes to avoid.	Student wrote 1-2 mistakes to avoid.	Assignment not done.

ALTERNATE ACTIVITIES for this lesson:
- Nuclear Bomb Chicken*
- Exaggerated Character Walk*
- Adverbilies*
- Ninja Star, Sleeping Kitten, Angry Chihuahua*

Lesson 7: Be in the Present

> *"If you're in your head, you're not here with me."*
> -Susan Messing, co-founder Annoyance Theater

OVERVIEW: As students begin to practice scene work, it is important to remind them that they need to stay in the present tense. One important aspect of being in the present is making strong initiations that tell the audience where the actors are and what they are doing. These initiations come in the form of verbal statements, pantomiming action or interacting with the environment.

Be: (verb) to exist

Present: (noun) the period of time occurring now

OBJECTIVE: Students will make strong initiations that are rooted in the present.

MATERIALS:
- Scene Openers copied and cut up into slips **(Appendix C)**
- Homework handout for each student **(Appendix B-1)**

GREETING:
- If homework was assigned:
  - *Does anyone have any thoughts on any of the videos that they watched last night?*
  - *In the scenes, were they talking about events that they did in the past or were they doing things in the present?*
- *Today we're going to explore what happens to our scenes when we talk about the past and future and how object work forces us to be in the present.*
- *Let's start with a warm-up.*

WARM-UP: Talking Heads
- Invite two students to stand on the stage.
- Get a suggestion of an action *(see **Appendix C**)*.
- Students stand in one place and talk about a time in the past when they did the suggested action.
- After a few minutes, call "scene," and invite two new volunteers to the stage. Get a suggestion of a location *(see **Appendix C**)*.
- Students stand in one place while discussing what they will do at the suggested location in the future.
- Edit the scene after a few minutes.
- **Game Debrief:** *How was it to "act" in one of these scenes? Was it easy to stand there and talk about things? What was the experience like as an audience member? Did it get boring?*

DISCUSSION:
- *Today we are working on being in the present in our scenes.*
- *This warm-up was an example of the opposite of what we want to do.*
- *As an audience we are not interested in watching actors talk about what they did or what they plan to do. We want to see them doing it and talking about it in the now.*
- *Object and environment work, along with pantomiming, are three ways of keeping your scene in the present. You can't be in the past when you are doing or expressing emotion about something in the present.*

- *If you are at a loss for what to do, start a physical action and commit to it.*
- *After some time either you will figure out what you are doing or your scene partner will endow you with a character that will explain your action. We call this giving your scene partner a gift, or gifting.*

ACTIVITY: Surprise Movement *[Video in Bonus Digital Material]*
- Have the students wander about the classroom space until you give a signal.
- At this point, they begin making a small physical gesture, such as bouncing a hand up and down or tilting their head over to their shoulder.
- They keep doing it over and over again until they figure out what they are doing.
- Call freeze.
- While everyone is frozen, ask a few students to repeat their movement and say what they are doing.
  - i.e. A student bouncing their hand might be dribbling a basketball or patting a small child on the head. A student bouncing their head might be dancing or could be a human bobble head.
- If students struggle to come up with something, ask their classmates to come up with an idea for them.
- Students return to wandering about and repeat this procedure two or three times.
- **Game Debrief:** *How long did it take you to figure out what you were doing? A great way to open a scene is to start with a physical movement. You may not even know what you are doing. Luckily, your scene partner can give you a gift by joining in with your movement and/or by using dialogue to justify the movement.*

DISCUSSION:
- *In improv scenes we want our dialogue to be filled with strong present tense statements.*
- *What do we think makes a statement strong?*
- *I will give you some examples of statements to compare. Listen and tell me which is stronger and why. Or, write these statements on slips of paper and hand to your students to read.*
- *"This is great!"* or *"This is the most delicious chili I have ever eaten."* (The 2nd one because it contains more details and is more specific).
- *"I want the red one daddy!"* Or *"I told you yesterday that I wanted the red robot daddy!"* (Although the 2nd statement has more details, it's in the past, which is a less strong choice).
- *"You were the worst tennis player in the tournament."* or *"You are the worst tennis player I have ever seen."* (First is again in the past. Second makes it your opinion which adds emotion, making it stronger).
- *Now it is your turn to come up with strong, in the present moment statements.*
- Ask the class to come up with a few examples of strong statements.
- *Let's practice as a group...*

> **Questions:** One rule of thought in improv is to never ask questions. The rule of not asking questions can be broken IF the question adds information to a scene and IF it is a question that your character would ask. "Is that your pecan pie, Mrs. Smith?" This lets us know who is being asked and that the scene involves pie. Younger students often need the rule to avoid questions, while older students should be made aware, that it can be broken if used judiciously.

ACTIVITY: I'm Coming Over for Pancakes *[Video in Bonus Digital Material]*
- The class stands in a circle.
- One at a time, students take turns making eye contact with players across the circle from themselves.
- As they walk towards that player to take their spot, they say the line, "I'm coming over for pancakes."
- Once everyone has gone at least once saying "I'm Coming Over for Pancakes," the game is open for students to create a new strong statement in the present tense, such as "These pants don't fit!" Or "This is the last time I ask you for help."
- Each time there is a new statement, every student should have the opportunity to say that statement.

- Note: If your group is very large, consider creating smaller groups of 8-10 players per circle.
- **Game Debrief:** *Were you surprised how many different ways there were to say the same phrase? If you came up with one of the statements, was it easy or difficult to make it present tense? Could you see a scene following any of these sentences?*

ACTIVITY: Bump, Set, Spike
- A classic volleyball technique is Bump, Set, Spike. One player bumps the volleyball into the air. A second player sets the ball up at the net. The first player spikes the ball across the net.
- We're going to use this idea to practice making statements in two-person scenes.
- Have the students form two columns on the stage.
- Round One - Bump Set:
  - A student from the stage left column walks forward and interacts with an object, the environment or pantomimes a motion.
  - Next, a student from the stage right column joins them in the action and makes a strong present tense statement that conveys what that action is.
    - *Example:* Stage left student steps forward, kneels and grabs something over their head.
    - Stage right student enters, kneels, grabs something over their head, and says, "I can't believe our miniature apple trees are finally growing fruit!"
  - Once the dialogue has been said, students return to the end of the opposite line.
  - Remind students the rule of teamwork and trying to make our scene partners look good. Actions should not be obscure. Remember to use associations and logical steps.
- Round Two - Bump Set Spike: (If you have a novice group, skip this round).
  - Place cut up slips of scene openers from **Appendix C** in a bowl. Set the bowl next to the stage right students.
  - A student from the stage left column steps forward and interacts with an object, the environment or pantomimes a motion.
  - Next, a student from the stage right column takes a slip of paper from the bowl, joins in the motion and reads the line of dialogue.
  - Finally, the stage left student justifies the statement with a reply.
    - *Example:* Stage left student steps forward, kneels and grabs something over their head.
    - Stage right student steps forward, kneels, grabs something over their head and reads from the slip of paper, "Mom, I need you to braid my hair."
    - Stage left student replies, "I will braid your hair as soon as we finish pulling these mice nests out of the fireplace flue."
  - Like in round one, students return to the opposite line.
- **Game Debrief:** *Which job was easier, making the physical choice or having to justify the action with a statement in the present? Always remember teamwork. If your partner is doing an action and you go to make a statement, make sure it is in the present and related to their action.*

WRAP-UP:
- *In that last game, the physical actions and present tense statements are what we call strong initiations.*
- *If we remember to start off all our scenes with strong initiations that happen in the now and utilize object and environment work and pantomimes, our scenes will have solid foundations to grow upon.*

Lesson 7: Journal Homework

Today we learned that scenes begin with strong initiations. These initiations are often present tense emotional statements. Tonight write a list of five powerful statements that could open a scene.

	3 Points	2 Points	1 Point	0 Points
RUBRIC	Student wrote a list of 5 strong opening statements.	Student wrote a list of 1-4 statements OR some of their statements were not strong.	Student wrote a list of 1-4 statements AND some of their statements were not strong.	Assignment not done.

Lesson 7: Video Homework

Tonight you will see why some improvisors say another rule of improv is "Make statements, not questions." As beginning improvisors we often get scared in a scene and ask our partner questions. When we do this, we force our partner to create things or worse yet, they turn the question right back on us and the scene doesn't go anywhere. Tonight's videos include one that shows questions leading a scene nowhere. The other shows how good improvisors use questions to further a scene (See Sidebar p 34). It also shows how hard it is to avoid statements. (Notice how many times actors get buzzed out of the game). In your journal list three examples of questions to avoid in scenes. (You will find these in the first video). Extra credit point if you come up with an example of a question that a character might use in a scene that includes information to further the scene.

The Rules of Improv: The "Questions Only" Improv Game
https://youtu.be/kH-_0sg_KMM

Whose Line Is It Anyway - Questions Only - International Flight (Starts at 50 seconds)
https://dai.ly/x55jdgt

	3 Points	2 Points	1 Point	0 Points
RUBRIC	Student wrote three examples of questions to avoid.	Student wrote two examples of questions to avoid.	Student wrote one examples of questions to avoid.	Assignment not done.

ALTERNATE ACTIVITIES for this lesson:
- Freeze*
- MacGyver**
- Goalie**

Lesson 8: Tell A Story (Part I)

> *"The world is made up of stories, not of atoms."*
> -Muriel Rukeyser, poet

OVERVIEW: One of the most important skills for improvisors to master is telling a story. Most problems in improv scenes come down to poor storytelling. In this lesson, you will teach your students the *Important Elements of Storytelling*. Advanced students will also learn more about playing the *game within the game*.

OBJECTIVE: Students will demonstrate the ability to tell a story with characters, locations, a beginning-middle-end, and a conflict.

MATERIALS:
- "Bad Stories" print outs **(Appendix B-2)**
- "Fairy Tale" print outs for each group (links listed below)
- "Conflict Handout" for each student **(Appendix B-3)**
- Stopwatch
- Homework handout for each student **(Appendix B-1)**

Tell: (verb) communicate information or give a narrative

Story: (noun) an account of imaginary or real people and events told for entertainment

GREETING:
- If homework was assigned:
  - Ask a few students to share their strong initiation statements from their homework.
  - How did the questions in the Whose Line video differ from the ones in the Rules of Improv video?
  - By only asking questions, it is difficult to move a story forward.
  - Good improv scenes tell a story.
- Today we will explore the Important Elements of Storytelling which help us create satisfying improv scenes.

WARM-UP: Bad Stories
- The following stories are each missing one major component of storytelling; characters, locations, beginning-middle-end, and conflict.
- These stories can be read in class or assigned as a homework assignment the night before.
- If reading in class, ask for six volunteers to come up and read a story to the class.
- Ask the class if they can figure out what element was missing in each story. Make a list.
- Briefly discuss how they would add in the missing elements. Let the class know that you will come back to these stories in the next lesson.

STORY 1: Francesco and the Rent Money
Once upon a time there was a boy named Francesco. Francesco lived in a small apartment in the city. One day he was finishing his breakfast when there was a knock at the door. It was his landlord Mr. Smith. Mr. Smith told Francesco that his rent was past due and that if he didn't pay by the next day he would be evicted. Francesco was terrified. He had blown all the money at the casino the night before. He had no

idea how he could come up with another $500 in one day. He felt relief as he handed the money to Mr. Smith and vowed never to gamble again.

Discussion:
- *This story is missing the middle. How did he come up with the money?*
- *If this were an improv scene, what would Francesco do? If I were in the scene I would have him running all over town doing silly acts to get money. Every character that Francesco ran into would have him do a dumber and dumber act.*

STORY 2: Go to Bed
It was a dark and stormy night. Someone was putting their kid to bed. Every time they left the room, the kid would sneak out and run back downstairs into the living room. On the third time that the kid snuck out of the room, the person was furious. "Go to bed!" they screamed as they chased the kid up the stairs. This time they knew what to do. They pulled out their drill and the lock they had been meaning to put on the door for months. Tonight was the night. They screwed the lock on the door, told the kid goodnight and slid the lock tight after closing the door. Five minutes later the kid tried to open the door to no avail. The kid screamed as loud as they could for five minutes and then passed out on the floor. The person quietly slid open the lock, opened the door enough to sneak in and carried the kid back their bed.

Discussion:
- *There are no defined characters in this story. A person and a kid are all that are mentioned. Is it a parent and child? A babysitter? A grandparent?*
- *Giving names makes improv scenes more relatable for the audience. (See Sidebar p 26).*

STORY 3: Martha and George and the Hot Date
Every Friday, Martha and George had a hot date. For 50 years of marriage they went to their favorite spot and ate dinner. This Friday was different. They showed up and the door was locked. How could this be? For 50 years they had come to this place and now, out of nowhere it was closed. George was furious, but Martha, always the calm one in the relationship, told her beloved husband that maybe after 50 years it was time for a change. They walked down the street to another place and walked in the door. Now was the time for a new tradition to begin.

Discussion:
- *We know who our characters are, but we have no idea where they are. It could be some sort of a restaurant, but there are no details.*
- *In improv, the humor in a scene like this is playing off the expectation that a hot date should be at a nice restaurant but maybe it is instead a fast food joint.*

STORY 4: Jeff and the Big Game
Jeff walked into the school gym filled with anxiety. He hadn't played a game since he had blown his knee. Would he be back to his star status? Could he lead his team to another state championship? He walked up to Mr. Salerno and said, "I'm ready to play coach." The coach was unsure if Jeff was ready to play, but their team was down 6 points and there was only 3 minutes left in the game. If anyone could bring the morale up, and lead this team to victory, it was Jeff. "OK kid," he said. "Get on the court." Jeff ran onto the court.

Discussion:
- *This story is missing the ending. What happened? Did Jeff score a few points? Did he get reinjured? Did he choke?*

- *In improv we often play the opposite of what is expected, Jeff could ruin the game for his team. He starts small by making a foul. Then he has an error. Finally he throws the ball in the opponent's basket to win the game for them.*

STORY 5: The Playground
Sylvia and Ivan loved to go to the playground together. The two siblings were two years apart, but were the best of friends. When they got to the park they threw their jackets off and immediately ran to the see-saw and hopped on. It was their favorite thing to do there. They bobbed up and down for what seemed like an eternity. The sun started to go down and they knew that their mom would be wondering where they were. They gathered their jackets and headed home.

Discussion:
- *We know that Sylvia and Ivan are siblings and that they are kids. We know where they are. We have a beginning, middle and end, but the story has no conflict.*
- *What if every piece of playground equipment was broken? What if they got severe injuries on each piece of equipment? Find a pattern of something going wrong and make it worse each time.*

STORY 6: Maria Goes to the Circus
Maria was in tears and on the verge of a temper tantrum. This was her reward for filling in her entire sticker chart for good behavior. It wasn't fair that her mother lost the tickets. She deserved to go to the circus. She worked hard. Finally, when they looked through the last kitchen drawer, underneath the take out menus, Maria's mother screamed, "I found them!" Crisis averted. Maria would get to go and see the clowns, elephants and trapeze artists after all.

Discussion:
- *This story is missing the beginning. We have no set up to who Maria is or why she is so upset.*
- *While this makes for a bad story to read, in improv it actually works. In improv we like to start in the middle of things. This way, we miss the boring lead up details and get to the heart of the story. If this were an improv scene, it could open with the strong initiation of the mother and Maria pantomiming tearing apart the apartment and Maria making the statement, "Mama, I can't believe you lost the tickets. I worked so hard for this!"*

DISCUSSION: Important Elements of Storytelling
- On the board write:

> ***Important Elements of Storytelling:***
>
> - *Characters*
> - *Locations*
> - *Beginning-Middle-End*
> - *Conflict*

- *All good stories, whether they are told in novels, plays, tv, movies or in an improv scene have certain elements in common.*
- *As we saw in the Bad Stories, if a story is missing an element, it falls apart.*
- *Today we will work as a team to make strong statements and associations and to "Yes, And" each other to create good stories.*

- *Listening to what others have added before us and relating to our scene partners is critical to creating cohesive stories that make sense.*

ACTIVITY: Ten Second Fairy Tale
- Divide the class into groups of 4-5 students.
- Assign each group a different fairy tale to perform. (See Links Below).
- Tell each group their goal is to perform the fairy-tale in under 60 seconds. Remind them that they must include the *Important Elements of Storytelling*.
- Allow for three minutes of practice. Then have each group share.
- Discuss the *Important Elements of Storytelling* after each performance.
- Once each group has performed, tell the class that they will perform the story again, but will only have 30 seconds.
- For the final round, they will have only 10 seconds.
- **Game Debrief**: *Stories are incomplete if they lack important elements. They can also drag on if they are filled with unimportant details. There is a sweet spot to performing an improv scene where you have just enough fun details to keep your audience entertained and all the important elements so they stay engaged.*

Links to Fairy-Tales

- *https://americanliterature.com/childrens-stories/the-three-little-pigs*
- *https://americanliterature.com/childrens-stories/little-red-riding-hood*
- *https://americanliterature.com/childrens-stories/jack-and-the-beanstalk*
- *https://americanliterature.com/childrens-stories/goldilocks-and-the-three-bears*

DISCUSSION: Conflict
- *Let's dive into the last element of storytelling a little deeper: Conflict.*
- *Without conflict, stories have no excitement.*
- *Literature and film conflict is often broken down into the categories that begin with "man versus..."*
- *Here are some examples of these.*
- Pass out Conflicts Handout **(Appendix B-3)**
- Read a few of the examples and discuss:
  - Man versus Self: Harry Potter: Hallows or Horcruxes?
  - Man versus Man: Hunger Games: Katniss killing other tributes.
  - Man Versus Society: The Grinch against the Whos.
  - Man Versus Nature: Hatchet: Brian versus the elements post plane crash; animal attacks, tornado, finding food, etc.
  - Man Versus Technology: Terminator and Westworld: Man versus Robots
  - Man Versus Fates/Gods/Supernatural: Lord of the Rings: Frodo struggles against the eye of Mordor to follow his destiny and destroy the ring.
- *These are examples of BIG conflicts.*
- *One of the ways that improv stories differ from television, film and books is that improv conflicts are usually based off everyday, mundane problems.*
- *I believe this is why improv is so enjoyable to watch.*
- *In our next activity we are going to brainstorm everyday conflicts.*

Teaching Improv - A Beat by Beat Book

ACTIVITY: Create a Conflict
- Allow students 3-5 minutes to work with partners/groups to come up with everyday conflicts that fit into each of the categories from the handout.
- Students must come up with at least one example for each category.
- Encourage students to avoid physical conflicts in "man versus man" because they typically turn into chaos on stage and aren't fun to watch.
- Share as a group.
- **Game Debrief:** *What categories were easiest to create conflicts for? What were hardest? We are going to keep these everyday conflicts in our heads as we move into our next game.*

ACTIVITY: Story Spine:
- Write the following prompts on the board.
  - Once upon a time…
  - Every day…
  - But, one day…
  - Because of that…
  - Because of that…
  - Because of that…
  - Until, finally…
  - And, ever since then…

> **Story Spine Example**
>
> "**Once upon a time** in the Denver Airport there was a girl named Susan. **Every day**, Susan worked the cash register at the Burger King, even though she hated it. **But one day**, an unknown stranger handed her a boarding ticket for a flight to New York City. **Because of that** she decided to follow her dream of auditioning for a soap opera. **Because of that** she tried out for General Hospital. **Because of that** she got a role as a nurse with an evil twin. **Until finally**, the writers decided to kill off her character. **And, ever since then**, Susan has been working at a McDonalds in Time's Square."

- Novice Version:
  - Use this game to demonstrate familiar patterns that stories follow.
  - The Story Spine helps create well-constructed stories with beginnings that establish a main character, locations, routines, events that break the routines; middles that show the consequences of breaking routines; climaxes that set the resolution to the story in motion; and the resolutions.
  - Read the above example to demonstrate how the prompt works.
  - As a class, come up with a new story following the prompts.
  - Finally, give the entire class the same location and character for "Once upon a time." Partner up students and allow 3-5 minutes to write a story with the spine in their journals. Reconvene and share.
  - **Game Debrief:** *Was it easy or hard to come up with ideas using this format? What part of the story was the hardest to come up with?*
- Advanced Version:
  - If your students are capable story tellers, use the Story Spine to discuss "playing the game within the game."
  - The example story has two "games" within it. The pattern that gets heightened is the dream of being in a soap opera. In order to heighten the story, I made associations of what happens on a soap

opera (lots of hospitals, evil twins, characters getting killed off). I then used those ideas to make Susan's boring life better and better. I broke the pattern by killing her off the soap opera and taking away her dream. The second game that I played was returning to where we started. Susan began the story working at Burger King and ended working at another fast food restaurant, McDonalds. As a class, use the story spine to create several stories, playing with creating patterns within the game and heightening them.
- **Game Debrief:** *What patterns did our class create?*

WRAP-UP*:*
- *Today we focused our attention on Important Elements of Storytelling.*
- *All good stories have these elements.*
- *While there is crossover from literature and film to improv, something that distinguishes improv scenes is the focus on finding the humor in the every day.*

Lesson 8: Journal Homework

Novice
Utilizing the Story Spine, write a story including all the Important Elements of Storytelling.

Advanced
Utilizing one of the conflicts you created in Create a Conflict, write a story including all the Important Elements of Storytelling.

RUBRIC	3 Points	2 Points	1 Point	0 Points
	Student wrote a story that included all the *Important Elements of Storytelling*.	Student wrote a story that missed one *Important Element of Storytelling*.	Student wrote a story that missed more than one *Important Element of Storytelling*.	Assignment not done.

Lesson 8: Video Homework

Video Assignment: Watch the Roman Improv Games clip. In your journal, list the characters, location and conflict.

Roman Improv Games: Speak in One Voice
https://youtu.be/hoTAziyhO7s

Additional Video: If you talked about playing the game within the game with your students, assign this additional video of Keegan Michael-Key discussing setting up the rules and then playing the game within those parameters.

The Off Camera Show: Keegan-Michael Key Has the Perfect Metaphor for Improv
https://youtu.be/coZARWbdNls

RUBRIC	3 Points	2 Points	1 Point	0 Points
	Student listed the characters, location and conflict.	Student listed the two of the three required items.	Student listed one of the required items.	Assignment not done.

Lesson 9: Tell a Story (Part II)

> *"Don't bring a cathedral into a scene. Bring a brick; let's build together."*
> -Del Close, co-founder iO

OVERVIEW: Part II of this lesson on *Telling a Story* gives students the opportunity to practice storytelling utilizing the skills we've been practicing so far: associations, "yes, and", listening, relating, being honest and in the present.

OBJECTIVE: Students will demonstrate the ability to tell a story with characters, locations, a beginning-middle-end, and a conflict.

MATERIALS:
- "Bad Stories" handout (**Appendix B-2**)
- Homework handout for each student **(Appendix B-1)**

GREETING:
- If homework was assigned:
  - *Would anyone like to share the story that they wrote for homework?*
- *Today we build upon the last lesson and practice the skill of incorporating storytelling into our improvised scenes.*

WARM-UP: Five Word Group Story
- Sit the class in a circle and come up with a list of five unrelated words (i.e. house, carrot, bag, locker, Halloween, ball, etc).
- The goal is for the class to come up with a satisfying, entertaining story, one sentence at a time.
- The teacher sets the tone with the first sentence.
- The story proceeds with each student in the circle adding one sentence.
- All five words must be included somewhere in the story and the story must also include all the *Important Elements of Storytelling*.
- Remind the class to stick to the main storyline. Do not get sidetracked with unnecessary details!
- **Game Debrief**: *Did we accomplish our goal? Often in an improv scene we have an idea of where we think it should go, but someone takes it to a completely different direction. Is this a good or bad thing? A skill that good improvisors work on is non-attachment. You create something, put it out there and let it go. If you try and drive an improv scene, it will seem forced and you will be breaking Rule Number 1: Teamwork.*

ACTIVITY: String of Pearls *[Video in Bonus Digital Material]*
- Ask seven students to take the back line.
- The students must tell a story, one sentence at a time, out of order, in seven parts.
- The first player to step forward begins the story by setting up the characters and location.
- The second player to join in tells the last line of the story.
- The remaining five players fill in the rest of the story.
- As each new person adds their sentence, the previous students repeat their sentences.
- Encourage students not to fill in the remainder of the story in order (i.e. NOT 2,3,4,5).

- **Game Debrief:** *How did that go? Was it easier to join in early or later?* (If you have any students who added in a crazy sentence to get a laugh, remind them of the Teamwork Side Rule: Don't try to be funny alone. See Sidebar). *Did our stories make sense?*

ACTIVITY: Slide Show *[Video in Bonus Digital Material]*
- This game starts with a suggestion for a location that you would (or would not) like to go on vacation.
- Groups of 5-7 students create tableaus that represent photos (slides) from a vacation to that location.
- You, the instructor (for novice groups), or a student (in a more advanced class), recount the adventures of their family vacation based on what is going on in each tableau.
- Assign a student to turn out the lights for five seconds. During this time the 5-7 students pose their bodies in silly or outrageous positions, then freeze.
- When the lights come back on, you (or an advanced student) explain what is going on in the slide, justifying the odd positions that the students are frozen in.
- Repeat for three more slides.
- The first slide should be the beginning of the vacation. (Set up characters and location). The second and third are the middle. (Create a conflict and heighten it). The fourth is how the vacation ended. (Solve the conflict).
- **Game Debrief:** *Did our vacation stories make sense? Did they each have a beginning, middle and end?*

ACTIVITY: Bad Stories Part II
- This is an extension to the game played in the last lesson.
- Partner up students and give them one of the bad stories **(Appendix B-2).**
- Their goal is to perform the stories in a scene, filling in the missing element of each story.
- Give students a few minutes of prep time to fill in the missing information (location, character, beginning-middle-end or conflict) and to outline the scene but not plan dialogue.
- Remind students when they perform to listen and relate to their scene partner to form realistic dialogue.
- Remind students to start their scenes with a strong initiation statement, like the ones practiced in the lesson on being in the present.
- **Game Debrief:** *Was it challenging filling in the missing details? Which performances were most entertaining and why?*

WRAP-UP:
- *In these past two lessons we focused on telling stories. Let's recap what we've learned so far...*
- *In improv we create stories through teamwork.*
- *Good dialogue and conflicts are created through strong initiating statements.*
- *The story moves forward through beginning, middle and end by players "yes, and"ing each other.*
- *Finally by listening and relating to our fellow scene-mates, we give nuance to a scene and make it interesting for an audience to watch.*

Teamwork Side Rule:

Don't try to be funny alone. When you purposefully go for a laugh in a scene, it often comes at the expense of the story and the other players in the game. If you are thinking of funny things to say, you cannot also be listening to and relating to your scene partners. The humor in improv comes from working together to create honest scenes that audiences can relate to. Once you set up those scenes, you can create humor naturally by committing to the characters, relationships and patterns that you have established.

Lesson 9: Journal Homework

For your journal assignment, grab a magazine or a book with lots of pictures. Open to a random page and pick out a picture. Using that image as an inspiration, write a story including the Important Elements of Storytelling.

Advanced Students:
Try to challenge yourself to create a pattern and play a game with your story.

RUBRIC	3 Points	2 Points	1 Point	0 Points
	Student wrote a story that included all the *Important Elements of Storytelling*.	Student wrote a story with one missing *Important Element of Storytelling*.	Student wrote a story with more than one *Important Element of Storytelling* missing.	Assignment not done.

Lesson 9: Video Homework

Watch the TEDx improvisation scene inspired by mayonnaise and puppy. Summarize the story. Include the main characters, the beginning, the conflict, the resolution of the conflict and the ending.

Advanced Group:
Extra credit point if you list at least one time the improvisors played the game within the game.

The art of improvisation - Rapid Fire Theater - TEDxEdmonton
https://youtu.be/d3TsyT_EDBc

RUBRIC	3 Points	2 Points	1 Point	0 Points
	Student wrote a summary including the main characters, the beginning, the conflict, the resolution of the conflict and the ending.	Student wrote a summary but was missing 1-2 key components.	The student wrote a summary but was missing more than 2 key components.	Assignment not done.

Key Components for Video Homework: The dad only made mayonnaise sandwiches because this was the family tradition. Sandra, the daughter was mad at this because she didn't like them and mayonnaise caused her mother to leave them. Sandra talks her father into leaving the mayonnaise behind and going to the grocery store where he discovers ketchup. Meanwhile the mother has answered a Craig's List ad for a man who would grant her every wish. Unfortunately the wishes only revolved around being fed grapes and the mother is now bloated due to all the grapes. The father's "dad sense" tells him that his wife is in trouble and so Sandra and the father go off to save her. They find the mother. The father tells her he has given up mayonnaise. The mother says that she actually dreamed of eating her grapes with mayonnaise. They get back together and the family ends up happy. There is also a brief introduction of a dog and Knife who is a hunchback who feeds her only grapes. The Game within the Game: Going from mayonnaise to ketchup, the mother only getting one type of food (mayonnaise or grapes), the mother actually desiring mayonnaise.

ALTERNATE ACTIVITIES for this lesson:
- Automatic Story Telling*
- Yes No Banana Please*
- Conducted Story*
- Lie to Me*
- Let's Not*
- Three Words: Why Sorry Oh*
- Half Life**

Lesson 10: Develop Relationships

> *"Know your scene partners. We don't talk to strangers. When's the last time you had a deep, interesting conversation with someone at a bus stop?"*
> -Ian Roberts, co-founder Upright Citizens Brigade

OVERVIEW: By this point in the course, we have hit all the major components needed to perform an improv scene. This last lesson before we jump into scene work explores the skill of developing relationships. Relationships add nuance to a story and are a great way to play the game within the game. In this lesson, students learn how to relate to other characters through status play.

Develop: (verb) to build up, grow or improve

OBJECTIVE: Students will explore how status affects relationships, and how this can be used to enhance a scene for comedic or dramatic effect.

Relationship: (noun) the way in which two or more people are connected

MATERIALS:
- Homework handout for each student *(Appendix B-1)*

GREETING: Today we are going to focus on the relationships that players have to each other.

WARM-UP: We Both Want The Same Thing
- In this game, two people perform in a scene, with both characters wanting that same thing.
- Get a suggestion for a "want" that an actor might have in a scene, such as "I want to get an ice cream cone" or "I want to clean my room."
- Get two volunteers to come to the stage to play out the scene.
- Round One: Tell them to play out the scene as complete strangers.
- Round Two: Ask for two new volunteers. Assign the students characters with the same implied status (but do not tell the students about status yet). Examples: best friends, siblings who get along all the time.
- Round Three: Ask for two new volunteers. Assign each student a character with implied high or low status. Examples: class bully and class victim or "overbearing" parent and "timid" child.
- Round Four: Use the same students as the last round. Same characters from the last scene but this time, the status roles are reversed. The bully is actually a wimp. The child tells the parent what to do and the parent listens.
- **Game Debrief:** *What was it like when you had complete strangers in a scene? What was it like when the players were close? Improv scenes are more interesting and easier to perform in when we assume our characters know each other and have some sort of a relationship. Did the dynamic change from round two to round three? How? What happened with our character dynamics in the final scene? Which scene was most enjoyable to watch?*

DISCUSSION:
- *In life there is something called status. A good definition of status is the power difference between two people. Those of higher status have some dominance over those who are of lower status. Lower*

status people act subordinate to those of higher status. This is an important element to understand as it can greatly enhance the characters dynamics in our scenes. Let's explore...

ACTIVITY: High/Low Status Walk
- Let students know they will be walking around the room acting either as high status or low status.
- Coach the students to act out various levels of their status:
  - High Status:
    - *Make eye contact with others, hold head high and steady, shoulders back, walk in straight lines. If someone is in your direct line of movement, do not step aside, bump into them.*
    - *When you stop, spread out your body, take up space.*
    - *When you speak, make strong statements, speak authoritatively and in complete sentences.*
  - Low Status:
    - *Do not walk in straight lines. Avoid eye contact with others, look down to the ground, move your head around looking in a jerky fashion, either be stiff or have hunched shoulders. Avoid bumping into others.*
    - *When you stop, take up as little space as possible. Breathe quickly or irregularly. Rub your face, scratch your head.*
    - *When you speak apologize for something and do not speak in complete sentences.*
- Assign half the students high status and the other half low status.
- Have students mill about for a minute or two as their status. Tell them to freeze and talk to whoever is next to them, regardless of status.
- Tell the class to freeze. Switch status. High is low and low is now high.
- Have students mill about for a minute or two as their new status. Tell them to freeze and talk to whoever is next to them, regardless of status.
- **Game Debrief:** *Which status did you prefer playing, high or low? What were your conversations like when you talked to someone of the same status as you? What was it like when you talked with someone of a different status?*

DISCUSSION: Relationships
- *Relationships and status are an excellent way to play the game within the game and make your scenes more interesting.*
- *One way to play with status is to take on the stereotypical roles (king being high status, court jester being low status) and exaggerate them to the umpteenth degree. The king takes on more and more authority. The court jester embarrasses themselves in worse and worse ways.*
- *While it is often funny to play high status versus low status, it is also enjoyable to have two characters of similar status trying to raise or lower themselves more than their scene partner. Let's explore...*

ACTIVITY: 10% More or Less Status *[Video in Bonus Digital Material]*
- Ask two players to take the stage.
- Give them a suggestion of an object, a location or an event.
- The first student starts small and talks about how great their "suggestion" is.
- The second student "yes, ands" by making their "suggestion" a little better.
- The two students go back and forth for several rounds following the pattern of making things better and better.
- Once they have a few minutes to one-up each other, call scene.

> **Example 10% More Status: Suggestion - Birthday**
>
> *Student A: Every year my mom makes me a Betty Crocker cake.*
> *Student B: Every year my mom makes me a homemade cake decorated with Superman.*
> *Student A: Well I have ALL the Super Friends on my cake.*
> *Student B: My cake has sparklers.*
> *Student A: My cake actually shoots out fireworks.*
> *Student B: My dad hires the guy who does the fireworks for the 4th of July to set up a full display after we eat the cake.*
> *Student A: After we finish our cake, we take rocket ship rides into orbit.*
> *Student B: Once the fireworks show is over, we take the family space shuttle to the International Space Station.*
>
> This example used associations to move in logical steps. Betty Crocker cake to homemade cake to simple decorations to elaborate decorations to sparklers to fireworks to big fireworks to rocket ships to space.

- Get two new volunteers and a new suggestion.
- After several rounds raising status, switch to lowering status.

> **Example 10% Less Status: Suggestion - Birthday**
>
> *Student A: My birthday was so lame we only played pin the tail on the donkey.*
> *Student B: Mine was even worse. We didn't have any tails to pin on the donkey, so we had to pull up blades of grass from the lawn and use our own spit to make them stick.*
> *Student A: My yard is so bad that we don't have any grass, so we couldn't even sit outside to eat cake.*
> *Student B: My mom didn't make any cake, but instead gave me some chewed gum with a candle in it.*
> *Student A: My dad told me I wouldn't get a candle, since I wasn't allowed any wishes this year.*
> *Student B: After I blew out my candle I had to grant my mom a wish, which was to leave her alone.*

- **Game Debrief:** *Which did you prefer, raising your status or lowering it? What association chains were made in this game? The idea of raising or lowering your status in relation to your conflict is a strategy that you can use to move a story forward and find humor while making your scene partner look good.*

DISCUSSION:
- Another way to play with status is to break the typical pattern and switch out status (as we did in the final round of our opening activity).
- The king takes orders from the court jester or the teacher cries as his students throw paper airplanes around the room.
- Before we start our next game, let's come up with a list of relationships that are usually associated with having a high/low status break. (Look to **Appendix C** for ideas).
- On our list, who is typically the high status and who is typically the low status?

ACTIVITY: Status Switch
- Ask two volunteers to take the stage.
- Endow them with a relationship from the class list.
- Give them a conflict that is based on the relationship.
  - Examples:
    - Teacher and student. The student doesn't understand the lesson.
    - Bank robber and bank teller. The robber demands all the money in the safe.
- Have the students start their scene playing the roles in traditional high/low status mode (i.e. Teacher and robber are high. Student and teller are low).
- Allow the students to establish their characters' status and go through a few rounds of heightening the conflict before editing the scene.
- Have them start over from the top, but this time they play their character with the opposite status (i.e. Teacher and robber are now low while student and teller are high).
- **Game Debrief**: *Were these scenes easier or harder to perform than others we have done? If so, why? What status did you enjoy playing more in these scenes? Did you prefer playing traditional status roles or the reversal?*

WRAP-UP:
- *Today we focused on bringing a little nuance to our characters and their relationships to one another through status.*
- *In improv, developing these relationships and playing off of them with high and low status adds a new dimension to your scenes.*

Lesson 10: Journal Homework

Come up with a list of three scenarios where high and low status could be played opposite or heightened for comedic effect. Example: The class bully and the class wimp, but instead of stealing lunch money the bully gives the money to the wimp.

RUBRIC	3 Points	2 Points	1 Point	0 Points
	Student listed three scenarios.	Student listed two scenarios.	Student listed one scenario.	Assignment not done.

Lesson 10: Video Homework

Tonight you will watch one improv scene and two sketch comedy pieces. After watching the first video, list three ways the actors raised or lowered their status. Next check out the two sketch comedy pieces. Sketches are usually developed after exploring ideas through improv scenes. The following sketches have good examples of both status play and playing the game within the game. Mr Show's "24 is the Highest Number" is a fantastic example of taking a ridiculous premise and running with it for comedic affect.

Slide Quest - Status Switch
https://youtu.be/Q4TaA_2ZW6o

Mr Show with Bob and David - Season 3 Episode 7 - "24 is the Highest Number"
https://youtu.be/RkP_OGDCLY0 (Full episode available on Amazon Prime. Sketch starts at 11:30)

Key and Peele - Substitute Teacher
https://youtu.be/Dd7FixvoKBw

RUBRIC	3 Points	2 Points	1 Point	0 Points
	Student listed 3 ways the players raised or lowered their status.	Student listed 2 ways the players raised or lowered their status.	Student listed 1 way the players raised or lowered their status.	Assignment not done.

ALTERNATE ACTIVITIES for this Lesson:
- You're Fired*
- Deck of Cards*
- Three Line Scene*
- Status Exercise*
- Always Never Also**

Teaching Improv - A Beat by Beat Book

Lesson 11: Two Person Scenes (Part I)

> *"Simple scenes are all you need; it doesn't have to be 'about' something."*
> -Greg Hess, Improvised Shakespeare Company

OVERVIEW: Two person scenes are the quintessential presentation of improv (for both short form and long form). When two people come to a stage, step into the moment and create a world that both players and audience become a part of, it is a beautiful thing. This lesson explores the skills necessary for a two person scene to be successful.

OBJECTIVE: Students will perform two person scenes that feature characters who have a relationship with one another, locations, a strong initiation that starts in the middle of the action, and a conflict.

MATERIALS:
- Two Person Scripts handout, one copy of each script **(Appendix B-4)**
- Two Person Scripted Scene Rubric for each student **(Appendix B-5)**
- Two Person Scene Grading Sheets for each student **(Appendix B-6)**
- Homework handout for each student **(Appendix B-1)**

GREETING:
- If homework was assigned:
  - *Does anyone want to share their status scenarios from last night's homework?*
  - *Any thoughts on any of the assigned videos?*
- *Today we are going to focus on the elements that make two person scenes successful.*
- *Do you remember the strong statements we made in the game I'm Coming Over for Pancakes?*
- *Improv scenes often start with strong initiation statements.*
  - *These statements tell us who the characters are, where they are and what they are doing.*
- Write on the board:

> **Qualities of Great Improv Scenes**
> 1. Location
> 2. Strong Initiation
> 3. Relationship
> 4. _____

- *We'll fill in the 4th blank in a bit. For our warm-up, we're going to focus on the first three on this list.*

WARM-UP: Where Have My Fingers Been *[Video in Bonus Digital Material]*
- *We're going to use our fingers to help us create fun scenes that incorporate location, strong initiations and relationships.*
- This game begins with a chant:
  - *"Where have my fingers been, I said where have my fingers been? Where have my fingers been, I said where have my fingers been?"*
- While everyone chants they bend their pointer fingers and sway them to the beat.

- Point to a student and assign them a location, such as a grocery store check out line or the elephant house at the zoo. (Be specific).
- The person assigned the location uses their fingers as puppets to create a three-line scene.
- Using the location as a starting point, they must make a strong initiation statement and establish a relationship.
- Example:
  - Entire Class: *"Where have my fingers been, I said where have my fingers been? Where have my fingers been, I said where have my fingers been?"*
  - Teacher points to a student and says: *"Playground at school."*
    - Student:
      - Finger One: *"Bobby, I double dare you to kiss Sarah behind that tree over there."*
      - Finger Two: *"Ricky, kissing girls is gross."*
      - Finger One: *"Well if you don't want to, then maybe I will."*
    - Entire Class: *"And that's where my fingers been. I said where have my fingers been..."*
- The chant continues and the student who created the last scene assigns a location to another student in the circle.
- Game continues until all students have the opportunity to create a scene.
- **Game Debrief:** *Was it easy or hard to create these 3-line scenes? What scenes were most successful and why?* (Had strong opening statements, characters had a relationship with each other, details, used location within their scene).

DISCUSSION: Qualities of Great Improv Scenes
- *Refer to the board again...*
- *Now, let's talk about what we're missing in that 4th blank spot for Qualities of Great Improv Scenes.*
- *As we covered in the lesson on "Telling a Story", what's missing?*
- *Conflict!*
- Add "conflict" to the list on the board.

> **Qualities of Great Improv Scenes**
> 1. Location
> 2. Strong Initiation
> 3. Relationship
> 4. Conflict

- *Review:*
  - **Location**: we need to know where you are.
  - Scenes need to open with a **Strong Initiation That Starts in the Middle of the Action**. Whether you start the scene with an action or a statement, make it a bold one.
  - Characters must have a clear **relationship** with one another. Your audience wants to buy into your scenes. In order to do that they need to know who you are and why you are together.
  - Finally, **Conflict**: Remember what we learned in storytelling. With no conflict there is no scene. Create a conflict and heighten it to move the story along.
  - To see what happens when one of these elements is missing, we're going to explore some pre-written two-person scenes.

ACTIVITY: Good Script/Bad Script
- Assign 5 pairs of students one of the scripts from **Appendix B-4: Two Person Scripts**.

- If you have remaining students, let them play "Where Have My Fingers Been" while the students with scripts practice.
- Scene 1 is an example of a "good" scene, containing all of the important components (strong initiation that starts in the middle of action, relationship, location, and conflict).
- Scene 2-5 are examples of "bad" scenes, in which one of those elements is missing.
- The students with Scene 1 should perform first
- Discuss the following points.
  - *What was the initiation (how the scene started) and why was it strong?*
  - *Did they start in the middle of the action?*
  - *What may have happened right before the scene started?*
  - *Where did this scene take place?*
  - *How do you know it is a kitchen?*
  - *Who was in the scene?*
  - *How were they related to one another?*
  - *What was the conflict?*
  - *What object work did they do in this scene?*
  - *How did it add to the scene?*
- Then allow the "bad" scenes to be performed, asking the same types of questions. Use the discussion notes (located with the stories in **Appendix B-4**) to identify what is missing from each scene and how it affected the performance.

DISCUSSION:
- *Now it is your turn to create and perform some scripted scenes that include the four Qualities of Great Improv Scenes and heightening through conflict and status.*
- <u>Advanced Groups</u>: *You should also create a pattern through conflict or status in your scene to heighten.*
- *Each student will get a rubric and a grading sheet to grade their own performance and their classmates' performance as well.*
- *Paying close attention to detail in others' performances gives us perspective and ideas for our own scene work.*
- *I will be the only one who sees these grade sheets.*

ACTIVITY: Partner Scripted Scene
- Partner up the students.
- Ask the students to look back in their journals at their lists of environments/locations from *Lesson 3: Yes, and...*and choose one to use for their scenes.
- Pass out the Two Person Scripted Scene Rubric and Grading Sheet to every student (**Appendix B-5** and **Appendix B-6**).
- Partners work together to write a short two person scene utilizing each of their characters from Lesson Six: Be Honest homework.
- Their scenes must include a location, a relationship between their characters, a strong initiation that starts in the middle of the action and a conflict.
- More advanced students should try to develop a pattern and heighten it to play the game within the game. That pattern can be within the conflict or play off of the high and low status of their characters.
- Scenes should be long enough to cover all the parts of the rubric.
- After each scene, students grade their classmates' performances, as well as their own, utilizing the rubric and the grading sheet.
- Collect the grading sheets.

- **Game Debrief:** *As a whole, how did our class do with their two person scripted scenes? What scenes did you like the most? Why?*

WRAP-UP:
- *Today we utilized all the skills we have developed over the past several lessons to perform scripted two person scenes.*
- *In the next lesson we will carry these skills into improvised two person scenes through a variety of short form games.*

Lesson 11: Journal Homework

Reflect upon your script and performance from today's lesson. What element was the easiest to come up with? Why? What was the hardest to come up with? Why? What do you feel your strengths are in improv? What areas do you want to improve upon?

RUBRIC	3 Points	2 Points	1 Point	0 Points
	Student wrote a reflection that included the easy and hard elements, strengths AND areas of improvement.	Student wrote a reflection that was missing one of the elements.	Student wrote a reflection that was missing more than one of the elements.	Assignment not done.

Lesson 11: Video Homework

Watch the following video clips of short form improv games. We will play versions of these in upcoming classes. Choose your favorite of the games and write at least three reasons why you liked it. Was it the format of the game? An actor's performance or character you to related to? The heightening of a pattern? Be specific as to why you enjoyed the scene.

Improv-A-Ganza: New Choice - Acrobatics (start the video at 1:45)
https://youtu.be/Mwra1FeNrS4

Four Square: The Second City Improv
https://youtu.be/hAmHgF21U-k

Jackson Adventure Video: The Laff Staff - Hijacked
https://youtu.be/wW8pkB93-dc

RUBRIC	3 Points	2 Points	1 Point	0 Points
	Student listed their favorite game and 3 specific reasons why they liked it.	Student listed their favorite game and 2 specific reasons why they liked it.	Student listed their favorite game and 1 specific reasons why they liked it OR they listed 2-3 reasons but the reasons were not specific.	Assignment not done.

ALTERNATIVE ACTIVITIES for this Lesson:
- Silent Scenes*
- Goalie**

Lesson 12: Two Person Scenes (Part II)

> *"Make your scenes a party onstage that the audience desperately wants to come to."*
> -Jorin Garguilo, CiC Theater and iO

OVERVIEW: Students now understand the concepts behind good two person scenes. In this lesson, students will practice those skills in classic short form improv games.

OBJECTIVE: Students will perform two person scenes that include characters who have a relationship with one another, locations, a strong initiation that starts in the middle of the action, and a conflict.

MATERIALS:
- Cut up slips of dialogue from **Appendix C** *"Opening Lines of Dialogue/Lines for Sentences"*
- Bowl or hat to contain the slips of paper
- Homework handout for each student **(Appendix B-1)**

GREETING:
- If homework was assigned:
  - *Does anyone have any thoughts on the videos that you watched last night for homework?*
  - *Which games did you like the most and why?*
- *Who can remind me of the 4 Qualities of a Great Improv Scene?*
  - Write them on the board:
  - 1) Location 2) Strong Initiation 3) Relationship 4) Conflict
- *Last class we wrote out two person scripted scenes that included these elements.*
- *Today we will work on adding those elements into improvised two person scenes.*

ACTIVITY: Four Square
- This is a game of rotating two person scenes.
- Two players stand next to each other downstage and two stand behind them upstage (making a square of players).
- The players move clockwise around the square when the teacher calls, "Switch right!"
- The downstage players are the ones who play the scene.
- Before starting any scenes, get suggestions from the class, based on the *4 Qualities of Great Improv Scenes* for each set of partners.
- Here are some suggestions:
  - Locations: an elevator, a phone booth, a tree house
  - A strong initiating statement: "I told you not to put that in your nose!"
  - Relationships: boss and employee, nurse and patient, astronaut and mission control
  - Conflicts: your car broke down, one of the players ran out of lunch money
- Once you have established the suggestion for each partnership, allow the first pair to begin a scene.
- Allow each partnership a minute or two to establish their scene before editing with a ring of the bell or a hand clap and "Switch Right!"
- Once each partnership has established their scene, the teacher can move through the scenes more quickly by calling to switch right or left. Repeated pairs should continue their scenes as they left off.

> **Note:**
> *This game is sort of a trial by fire that students will most likely struggle with in the beginning. Like any skill though, it will get better the more they practice. Feel free to jump in and coach/assist until the students feel comfortable.*

- End the game (if possible) on a laugh.
- Repeat with a new "four square" of students.
- <u>Advanced Level:</u> After scenes are established, call out "Firedrill!" Students run around for a moment, stopping in one of the four spots. Students play their original characters when they are in downstage right or left spots regardless of who their new partner is. The fun in this version is watching improvisors renegotiate who they are in relation to their new partner, location, etc.
- **Game Debrief:** *What did you like most about this game? What did you like least?*

ACTIVITY: Sentences
- This game requires a bowl filled with slips of random dialogue. Create these ahead of time using the *List of Opening Lines of Dialogue/Lines for Sentences* in **Appendix C,** *or by having students write down strong statements.*
- Ask two volunteers to take the stage.
- Their goal is to create a scene that at random times incorporates the slips of dialogue.
- To begin, grab a slip of dialogue from the bowl and read it out loud. This is the inspiration for the scene.
- Remind students to use object and environment work in their strong initiations.
- As the scene develops, randomly call out "Line." At this point, students must pause, grab a slip of dialogue, say the line and then justify it within the context of their scene.

Example: Teacher Reads Initial Slip: "No more stealing my peanut butter."

Student A: Billy, I don't want to swap lunches with you today.
Student B: We swap lunches everyday. I've gotten used to the way your mom cuts off the crust.
Student A: Well, my mom yelled at me last night when she found out I was giving you my PB&J and you were giving me your Twinkies.
Teacher: Line.
Student A: She said (pull out slip of dialogue) 'Stop kicking everyone in the shins.' You know what sugar does to me? If I don't eat my protein I just start kicking people and I'm gonna get expelled."
Student B: I get it, but it makes me so sad that my dad only packs me Twinkies for lunch.
Teacher: Line.
Student B: The other day I said to him, (take out slip of dialogue) 'You are the funniest member of our family', but Twinkies aren't funny anymore dad. So you know what he did? He packed me Ding Dongs instead."
Student A: Why didn't you say so? I love Ding Dongs so much more than Twinkies. In fact the first time I had one I shouted...
Teacher: Line.
Student A: (Pull out slip of dialogue) This year Arbor Day is going to be magical!' And every year since we have celebrated Arbor Day with Ding Dongs.

- **Game Debrief:** *How did these scenes go? Was it easier or harder to perform a good scene when you were also playing a game? Were these scenes more or less enjoyable to watch than the ones we have been performing without gimmicks?*

ACTIVITY: New Choice
- Ask players to take the stage and get a suggestion from the class for inspiration.
- Players begin a scene.
- Once the scene gets going, the teacher uses the bell to "ding" (or just clap) the player who just spoke and say "New choice."
- The student must change whatever it was they just said or did.
- Teacher can "ding" the student once and let them move on or continue making them come up with new things to say or do.
- Example:
  - Student A: "How many times do I have to tell you Jenny, this is not your bike." (Ding - new choice) "This is not your motorcycle." (Ding - new choice) "This is not your jet ski." (Ding - new choice) "This is not your pogo stick. (Student A starts pantomiming bouncing on a pogo stick). In fact, I got it for my birthday two years ago."
  - Student B: "Jack, you and I both got pogo sticks for OUR birthday. We are twins, we always get the same thing." (Ding - new choice) "We are triplets and two of us always get the same thing while the third doesn't get anything."
  - Student A: "Yeah, that year you were left out."
- **Game Debrief:** *What did you like most about this game? What did you like least? Was it hard to come up with new choices? Did our groups create characters, locations, relationships and conflicts?*

WRAP-UP:
- *Many of the most popular short form improv games are rooted in two person scenes.*
- *When we perform these games we need to remember to always incorporate the Qualities for Great Improv Scenes that make the scenes worth watching in the first place.*

Lesson 12: Journal Homework

Tonight write a short reflection about your biggest successes in today's scenes and mention at least one thing you struggled with. What could you practice to work on that struggle?

	3 Points	2 Points	1 Point	0 Points
RUBRIC	Student wrote a reflection including successes and one area of struggle. They listed something they could work on.	Student wrote a reflection including successes and at least one thing they struggled with but did not come up with something to practice.	Student wrote a reflection including successes OR one thing they struggled with AND did not come up with something to practice.	Assignment not done.

Lesson 12: Video Homework

Video Homework: Tonight's video homework gives you a sneak peak at how scenes with more than two players work. You have already seen the Armando. This time, I want you to focus on the dynamics on stage when there are more than two performers in a scene. Skip past the monologues to the scenes. Write three observations you made about the performances in the Armando or the Whose Line Is It Anyway group scenes.

Laff Staff: Armando
https://youtu.be/bPqX4H3qGFw?t=138

Whose Line is it Anyway: Old Job, New Job - Undertake Used to be a Used Car Salesman
https://youtu.be/l4fwDNWuUto

Whose Line is it Anyway: Superheroes - There's a Dead Possum in his Parking Spot (start at 0:45)
https://bit.ly/2tUtQvo

RUBRIC	3 Points	2 Points	1 Point	0 Points
	Listed three observations.	Listed two observations.	Listed one observation.	Assignment not done.

ALTERNATE ACTIVITIES for this Lesson:
- Alphabet***
- Hi-jacked*
- Zone-Ra***
- Puppets**
- Two Headed Scene**
- Ping Pong***
- Audience Add-Ins (Three Letter Acronym, Sentences, Sound Effects, Pillars, What's Text?, What's Next Charades?)***

Lesson 13: Group Scenes

> *"You don't go out there to sound good. You go out there to make everybody else sound good."* -Miles Davis

OVERVIEW: Now that your students are comfortable with two person scenes it is time to teach them how to play with three or more improvisors at a time. Group games can be a ton of fun. They are also a great way for less comfortable performers to be in a scene without taking on a main role. Group scenes require a new set of rules in order to avoid chaos.

OBJECTIVE: Students will explore how to effectively perform in scenes with three or more players.

MATERIALS:
- Bell
- Print outs of **Appendix B-7: Group Scenes**
  - Scene #1: 3 Copies
  - Scene #2: Each line cut into individual slips
  - Scene #3: 6 Copies
- Homework handout for each student **(Appendix B-1)**
  - Includes the End of Course Game Survey (see Journal Homework at the end of this lesson)

GREETING:
- If homework was assigned:
  - *Did you notice any differences between two person scenes and the group scenes?*
- *Today we will explore how to perform on stage with three or more improvisors in a scene.*
- *To warm-up, let's play a twist on an old game that incorporates all of the rules we have learned so far about storytelling and creating great scenes.*

WARM-UP: Alphabet Group Story
- Class starts in a circle.
- The goal is to tell a coherent, group story (similar to *Five Word Story* from *Lesson Five*).
- The twist is that each new sentence must start with the next letter of the alphabet.
- Get a suggestion for the story. *(See Appendix C)*
  - Example: Suggestion: vacuum cleaner
  - Teacher: "**A**lastair was known throughout his school as the human vacuum cleaner."
  - Student A: "**B**oys and girls alike were amazed by his ability to inhale food."
  - Student B: "**C**hewing was not something Alastair needed to do."
  - Etc.

DISCUSSION:
- *We just made a group story utilizing our improv rules.*
- *Now we are going to work on group scenes.*
- *What are some benefits and possible pitfalls of having more than three people in an improvised scene?*
  - Another person to come up with ideas.
  - Two players can play straight to one person playing a heightened character.

- Too many conflicting characters.
- Hard to keep track of what is going on.
- People talking over each other.
  - *In order to make group scenes work, we need to follow all the old rules we've learned, but also consider some new ones.*
  - Write the bolded rules below as you discuss.

#1: **Do not enter a scene unless you will add to it.**
  - *Only enter a scene if you can heighten what is going on.*
  - *Go in with a specific intent.*
  - *If two characters are discussing a third character and the third character would add to the scene, then enter as that character.*
  - *Let's see how this could play out:*
  - Ask 3 players to the stage and have them read through **Scene #1 from Appendix B-7: Group Scenes.**
    - *How did the mom add to that scene?*
    - *Where could the scene have gone from there?*
    - *Let's try out another scene.*
  - Ask 7 students to take the stage. Hand each a slip of dialogue from **Scene #2 from Appendix B-7: Group Scenes.**
    - Have them read their instructions and perform the scene in order.
    - After Student C says "Hey guys. What's happening?" freeze the scene.
    - *Did that character add to the scene? No. Entering a scene because you want to be on stage does not help make a scene better. Let's continue the scene and see how the next set of students create a pattern and heighten it.*
    - Have the scene continue.
    - Once the last student says their line, call "Scene."
  - *What those players did was called a walk-on. In a walk-on, you enter, give a strong offer that adds to the scene and exit. These are great and fun ways to add variety to a scene.*
  - *Sometimes you'll have several players start on stage at the same time. When this happens, we need to be aware of two more rules....*

#2: **Relationships Relationships Relationships**
  - *Play off the relationships in groups.*
  - *If two people establish themselves as parents, become their children OR act as another set of parents.*
  - *If two people are coworkers, become the boss.*

#3: **If there are more than three players in a scene, become part of the scenery or clump.**
  - *It gets very chaotic and hard to follow if you have five different characters with distinct personalities and different agendas.*
  - *Here are two options:*
    - *#1 Become part of the environment.*
      - *If the characters are at a farm, become a chicken pecking at the ground. If they are at a beach and mention palm trees, become a palm tree swaying in the wind. (Remember the Martha Game from Lesson 6: Be Honest).*
    - *#2: If you jump in as a character, align yourself with another established character.*
  - *Let's do one last scene.*
  - Ask 6 students to take the stage. Pass out scripts for Scene #3 from **Appendix B-7.**

Teaching Improv - A Beat by Beat Book

- Have them perform the scene.
  - *How did those players clump?*
  - *Notice how you can be onstage supporting the scene without adding lines to it.*
  - *Without the giggling girls, the conflict of asking out Becky would not have seemed as difficult.*

DISCUSSION:
- *Let's move onto some improvised group scenes.*
- *Our first game is one you saw in the homework, Old Job New Job.*
- *This game covers the first two rules. Do not enter until you are called for and make sure to develop relationships.*

ACTIVITY: Old Job New Job
- Ask three volunteers to take the stage.
- From the class, get suggestions for two very different jobs. Write them on the board and label one of them "New Job" and one of them "Old Job."
- Two students start the scene at the workplace of the new job.
- After a few minutes of establishing their relationship and the workplace, the third player enters.
- They are the "new guy on the job," but they keep doing the new job in the style of their old job.
  - Example:
    - New Job: Eye Doctor. Old Job: Librarian.
    - Ideas: First two students are a nurse and a patient. The Doctor enters and tells the other players to be quiet. They file eye glasses in a card catalogue. Instead of an eye chart they have the patient read Dewey Decimal numbers.
  - **Game Debrief:** What worked well? What didn't work well?

DISCUSSION:
- *We are now going to move onto a game where we play many scenes based off of one suggestion.*
- *The scenes start with one player and eventually end up with five improvisors on stage.*
- *Remember to "clump" when you get into four or five on stage.*

ACTIVITY: The Onion
- Ask 5 students to take the stage and from a back line.
- Get a suggestion for the scenes *(see Appendix C)*.
- Players create individual scenes based on the suggestion.
- Each scene is unrelated and should take the suggestion in a different direction with new and different characters.
- The game starts with one player stepping forward and performing a one person scene based on the suggestion.
- Once they have time to establish who they are and how the suggestion is tied into their scene, a second student steps forward and initiates the second scene.
- This new scene is based off the same suggestion, but takes the suggestion in a different direction.
- Once the relationship, location and conflict are established in this scene, a third player comes forward and begins a new scene with new characters, etc.
- This routine is followed for the fourth and fifth players.
- Once all five players are involved in a scene, the last player to join comes up with an excuse to exit the stage.
- The four player scene resumes.
- Students quickly resolve the conflict and the fourth student finds a reason to exit.
- This pattern continues until the original player is left on stage to conclude their one person scene.

- Teacher calls "Scene."
- Run the game with five new players if time allows.
- **Game Debrief:** *What worked and didn't work? Was it challenging to make a commitment to step forward and initiate? Did you trust that your group would have your back to make your scene work?*

WRAP-UP:
- *Today we learned some new rules for performing scenes with three or more improvisors.*
- *In our next lesson we get more chances to play with multiple people on stage and will add the element of guessing.*
- *Guessing games are some of the most beloved short form games in performances.*

Journal Homework: Create an End of Course Game Survey for your students. This is a list of every game you have played to date in class. List warm-ups separately. Attach this list to the homework handout.

Lesson 13: Journal Homework

<u>Directions</u>: *Attached to this handout is a list of all the games we have played in class. Circle your favorite warm-up game. Rate every other game on a scale of 1-3. This is how games for the performance will be chosen.*
1 = Disliked it
2 = Liked It
3 = Loved It.

RUBRIC	3 Points	2 Points	1 Point	0 Points
	Rated every game and circled the games they wanted to play.	Rated most games and circled the games they wanted to play.	Rated some games and/or didn't circle games they wanted to play.	Assignment not done.

Lesson 13: Video Homework

Watch the following clips of guessing games to prepare for the next class. List three things you noticed the endowed performers do that made it possible for the guessing player to guess.

Laughing Stock Improv: Late for Work (skip to 15:08)
<u>https://youtu.be/MpH5R-7a4i0?t=906</u>

Whose Line Is It Anyway: Party Quirks (Skip to 15:32 - 18:15)
<u>https://bit.ly/2UNzDhs</u>

RUBRIC	3 Points	2 Points	1 Point	0 Points
	Listed three things.	Listed two things.	Listed one thing.	Assignment not done.

ALTERNATE ACTIVITIES for this Lesson:
- Boom Chicago**
- Same Opener, Different Scene**
- Superheroes***
- Musical Chairs***
- Characters and Objectives**
- Foreign Film***

Lesson 14: Guessing Games

> *"When you come out as a standup, you get the feeling from a crowd - it's a kind of a 'make me laugh' attitude. But when you come out as an improvisor, they realize that they're suggesting everything you do. So they're already invested in the scene, and they actually want it to work."* -Ryan Stiles, Whose Line Is It Anyway

OVERVIEW: Guessing games are some of the most fun to watch as an audience and can be some of the most stressful, but exhilarating to perform in as an improv actor.

OBJECTIVE: Students will learn how to improvise within the structure of guessing games.

MATERIALS:
- Bell
- Homework handout for each student *(Appendix B-1)*

GREETING:
- *Today we will play guessing games.*
- *Guessing games are improv games in which players must guess some attribute of their fellow players.*
- *You have already placed a guessing game, LECI, in Lesson 4: Listening.*
- *While these games can be stressful, they are also some of the most fun to play.*
- *The audience becomes engaged because they take the side of the guesser(s). They are rooting for us.*
- *Most importantly, they find it absolutely mind blowing when we do figure it out.*
- *What they don't realize is, there are strategies involved in guessing games that help us out.*
- *Thankfully, you already have most of these strategies down. They are the same strategies that help us make great improv: listening, relating, and honest, present-moment pantomiming skills.*
- *Let's warm-up using some of those techniques...*

WARM-UP: What's My Job
- Have the class stand in a circle.
- Students take turns pantomiming actions performed in specific jobs while explaining the action in gibberish.
- The class guesses the job.
- <u>Example</u>: Short Order Cook - flipping pancakes and cracking eggs into a pan while explaining in gibberish "Blah blue blah goo bah, dah da."
- Go around the circle, allowing each student a turn.
- **Game Debrief:** *What was successful, what was not?*

DISCUSSION:
- *When we perform in guessing games, we need to be as specific as possible with our pantomiming.*
- *Specificity helps our teammates make better guesses.*

Guess (verb): *to form an opinion or answer without sufficient information to be sure of being correct*

Game (name): *an activity involving skill, played according to rules for amusement or fun*

ACTIVITY: Late for Class
- Ask 4 volunteers to take the stage.
- One student, the guesser, leaves the room.
- The other three students are classmates who stand together on one side of the stage.
- Ask the audience for three excuses as to why the guesser is late for class
  - i.e. lost their dog, flipped their car into a ditch, spilled hot chocolate all over their clothes, etc.
- You, the instructor, play the role of the principal and stand with your back to the classmates.
- Call in the guesser and demand to know why they are late for class.
- The classmates, behind your back, pantomime the first of the three reasons why the guesser is late.
- The guesser speculates their reasons based on the pantomimes.
- The principal's job (your job) is to keep the guesser on track.
- Give them hints if they are close ("Well that almost sounds likely, but not entirely") or let them know if they are way off ("There is no way that could happen").
- Every now and then turn around to check on their classmates. They freeze in whatever position they are in. Most likely it will be a bizarre position, such as crawling on the floor looking for a lost contact lens. The classmates justify their positions to the principal. ("We spilled the paper clip container!")
- Once the student gets the first excuse right, the principal accepts the excuse, but demands to know what else kept them from class.
- The classmates move on and pantomime the 2nd clue.
- Remind them to work together and if something isn't working, try a different approach.
- The game ends when the guesser says all three excuses.
- **Game Debrief:** *Was this easy or challenging? What techniques did you find to be most effective?*

ACTIVITY: Party Quirks
- This is the quintessential improv guessing game.
- Ask four volunteers to take the stage.
- One student is the guesser/party host.
- The others are party guests who have odd quirks that the guesser must figure out.
- The host leaves the room while the class gives each guest their endowment.
- While there are many ways you can create endowments for this game, I find it best to choose three "types" ahead of time so that the guesser has an idea of what they are looking for. I like to use:
  - Celebrity with a new job (Arnold Schwarzenegger as a zoo keeper)
  - Superhero with a fear (Wonder Woman who is afraid of cats)
  - Animal with a talent (elephant who can spin plates)
- Call the host back in and have guests step to the side of the stage.
- The game begins with the host setting up for the party and one guest knocking at the door.
- The first guest enters in character, dropping hints as to their endowment.
- After a few lines of dialogue, the next guest comes to the door and the host and new guest interact.
- Finally, the last guest enters.
- All guests and hosts should interact with each other, but not speak over each other. (Remember this is a group scene).
- As soon as the host guesses who a guest is, they call them out and that guest finds an excuse to leave.
- Game ends when the last guest is figured out.
- If the host cannot figure out who someone is, the teacher can knock on the door and enter as a delivery person, dropping as many hints as they can.
- <u>Easier Options</u>:

Teaching Improv - A Beat by Beat Book

- Hand out a slip of paper with a Party Quirks Endowment to each student. Allow 5-10 minutes for students to wander around the room talking to each other in character. Gather the class in a circle and ask students to guess their classmates endowments.
- Play a few "open" rounds of Party Quirks where the host knows who every guest is, but they still play in character, dropping hints.
- **Game Debrief:** *What strategies did you use to fully become your endowed character? As the party host, what did guests do that was most helpful for you?*

WRAP-UP:
- *Guessing games require using all the rules that we have learned.*
- *We need teamwork to help the guesser out.*
- *Associations are how we come up with hints.*
- *We accept the endowments/suggestions we are given and run with them (Yes, and).*
- *It is essential to listen and relate to those giving clues.*
- *We must be honest and clear with our clues or they will not be guessed.*
- *A big part of being in the present is working with objects and the environment.*
- *We tell stories through our clues.*
- *Finally, we can use relationships as a way to bring clarity to the characters we are representing.*
- *Pull out your End of the Course Game Survey (Homework assignment from Lesson 13).*
- *Please add today's guessing games to the list.*
- *Rate each game similar (on a scale of 1-3) and circle any you would be interested in playing in the performance.*
- *Hand in your Game Survey before you leave.*

Lesson 14: Journal/Video Homework

Your homework tonight is to watch more improv. Search youtube.com for Improv-A-Ganza, Whose Line Is It Anyway, and Laughing Stock TV for ideas of professional short form improv games and shows. If you search high school improv you will find examples of students your age performing. Write a short reflection about one of the videos that you watched. Include the URL, name of video, what you liked or didn't like about the game/performance.

	3 Points	2 Points	1 Point	0 Points
RUBRIC	Student wrote a short reflection of their video, including an explanation of what they liked or didn't like.	Student wrote a short reflection of their video but it was missing an explanation of what they liked or didn't like.	Student listed the name of a video but it did not include a reflection.	Assignment not done.

ALTERNATIVE ACTIVITIES for this Lesson:
- Interrogators***
- $5 Pyramid*
- Hint Away*

Lesson 15: Practice for Performance & Creating a Line-Up

> *"You're only limited by your lack of imagination and fear of appearing stupid."*
> -Susan Messing, co-founder Annoyance Theater

OVERVIEW: Getting students prepared for their performance by practicing the games you intend to play is essential. Practice not only gets students at ease in their roles, it also shows them how much everyone has learned over the course of the class.

Line-Up: *(noun) a list of participating players in a game, together with their positions*

Prior to this class, go through the End of the Course Surveys (they should have been handed in at the end of the last lesson), choose one warm-up and decide which games you will likely use in the final performance based on the students' responses. See the section below titled **"Putting Together a Line-Up"** to help you prepare for this session.

OBJECTIVE: Students will become familiar with the line-up of games and practice for their final performance.

MATERIALS:
- Stopwatch
- Bell
- Homework handout for each student *(Appendix B-1)*

GREETING:
- If homework was assigned:
  - *Who would like to share any thoughts on the video clips that you watched?*
- *Today, in preparation for our performance, we are going to run through several games that you indicated as your favorites.*
- *While each student will not be in all of their favorite games, I did my best to ensure you are in games that you enjoyed and/or will perform well in.*
- *In this class, I will be timing the games and seeing how different groups work together.*
- *I will determine our final line-up based on timing and group dynamics.*
- *I will try my best to put you in games that you gave preference to and that you practice in today, but no promises!*

WARM-UP:
- Start with a favorite warm-up from the End of the Course Survey.

RUN GAMES:
- Prior to this class, look through the End of Course Game Surveys filled out by the students.
- Prepare a Line-Up based on student interest and ability. (See *Putting Together a Line-Up* below for instructions on how to do this).

Teaching Improv - A Beat by Beat Book

- Run each game with the students who will likely perform in them, but understand that group dynamics or ability may cause you to change things up in the final line-up.
- Time each game to get an idea of how long it may run during the show.
- With a younger or more inexperienced group, you introduce each game in the show.
- With an older or more advanced group, allow students to introduce each game in the show.
- You edit all scenes, but can have students working lights and or sound. (See below for more info).

WRAP-UP:
- *How are people feeling about the upcoming performance?*
- *It is typical to be a bit nervous. After all, we will be creating a performance with no script.*
- *However, remember, you have all the skills necessary to perform great improv.*
- *Remind yourself of the rules, and harness that nervous energy into an unforgettable performance.*

Putting Together a Line-Up

What is a line-up? Simply put, it is a list of the games that are played in a show and who plays them. When putting together the line-up for your class performance take into account the following pieces of information. (See **Appendix D: Sample Line-Ups** for examples).

INTRODUCTIONS:
- Keep introductions simple.
- For most games, follow this simple procedure:
  - 1) Ask the the players to take the stage.
  - 2) Ask for a "get" or suggestion for what the scene will be about. (See **Appendix C** for ideas).
  - 3) Then introduce the game with the title and the suggestion.
- Example:
  - "Let's bring out the players for this next game." (Players come out). "What is something I might find in my junk drawer?" (Audience calls out ideas. Person doing intro chooses one suggestion). "This game is String of Pearls: Rubber Band."
  - If the game has a gimmick, give a brief explanation before saying the game title and suggestion. i.e. "Whenever I ding this bell and say, "New Choice" the actor must pick a new thing to say or do. This is New Choice: Rubber Band."
  - Some games require specific "gets" such as Slide Show (location) or Four Square (different gets for each partnership).
  - For guessing games, first send out the guessers, then ask the audience for the items needed.
  - Check out Improv-A-Ganza videos for ideas on how to introduce games and get suggestions:
    - *https://www.youtube.com/user/improvftw*

EXPERIENCE LEVEL
- This is broken into three levels.
- If your entire class falls into one of these categories, use only games from that group and/or add in ones from a level below.
- If you have a mixed experienced group (as will be the case for most classes), classify your students and put them into games reflective of their level.

- **Novice:** Young, immature or haven't had enough practice to hold up a two person scene. Involve these students in simple and low risk group games.
- Sample of Novice games:

- 3 Some
- Great Machine
- Translate Gibberish
- 10 Second Object
- Complementing Actions Game
- Rumors
- Yes, Let's
- Conducted Story
- Yes, and
- Luckily Unluckily
- Translate Gibberish
- The Oracle
- Adverbilies
- Martha Game (without adding in opposite characters)
- Ten Second Fairy Tale (perform the ones they did in class)
- Slide Show (teacher runs the slideshow)

- **Intermediate:** Have a solid understanding of the rules of improv. Feel comfortable adding to a story, but are not strong enough to hold up a two person scene. Sample of Intermediate games:
  - Hi-Jacked
  - Rumors
  - Madison Avenue,
  - Two Headed Interview
  - Five Word Group Story
  - Alphabet Group Story
  - Slide Show (let strong improvisors tell the story)
  - String of Pearls
  - Freeze
  - MacGyver
  - Superheroes
  - Late for Class
  - Martha Game (with someone coming in as opposite character)

- **Advanced:** Have a solid understanding of the rules of improv and are comfortable in two person and group scenes. Sample of Advanced games:
  - Sentences
  - New Choice
  - Ping Pong
  - The Onion
  - Musical Chairs
  - Forward Reverse
  - Half Life
  - Four Square
  - Three Letter Acronym
  - Sound Effects
  - Alphabet
  - Zone-Ra
  - Puppets
  - Two Headed Scene
  - Old Job New Job
  - Party Quirks
  - Interrogators
  - Freeze

STUDENTS
- First and foremost, look to the games your students say they want to play.
- If they are capable of playing those games, sign them up.
- Audiences delight in watching students enjoy themselves on stage.
- Some students will never be comfortable in front of an audience. Make sure there are options available where they can perform, but will not feel the pressure of being in the spotlight. Group games and novice level group games, like 10 Second Object and Slide Show are great for this.

CLASS SIZE
- If you have a class of 20, put in large group games to accommodate each student getting stage time.
- If you have a class of 8 advanced students, make sure each of them get a two person or three person scene in addition to other group games.

PACING
- The goal is to keep your audience hooked and your students engaged and involved.

- Start with a high energy game that involves a lot of students (10 second Object, Hi-Jacked, Freeze), then segue into to more mellow, smaller games (Conducted Story, Group Stories, any two person scene game, etc).
- Continue to mix this up throughout, finishing up with a big group game (Slide Show, Freeze).
- Look to *Appendix D: Sample Line-Ups* for pacing ideas.

PERFORMANCE TIME
- Depending on class size, anywhere from 30 minutes to an hour is a solid show.
- Game times can obviously vary. Don't feel bad editing a game quickly and moving on if it feels like the scene is not going anywhere.
- Check times during prep before finalizing the line-up.

SOUND AND/OR LIGHTS
- Sounds and Lights are a good way to get students involved in the show in a non-performance role.
- If you plan on using students for sound and music, train them before the practice for the performance.
- If you are in a theater, train students how to run the booth. If you are in a classroom, assign one student to lights (stand at the light switch) and another to music. (They sit to the side with a sound system. This can be as simple as a phone and bluetooth speaker).
- Each time the teacher yells "Scene," the lights get turned off and the music person plays 20-30 seconds of music. Cheesy pop hits are a good choice. The teacher or a student create the playlist prior to the practice.

For the Teacher: Hand out a copy of the list of "Gets" from *Appendix C*. Read through this list of "Gets" which are questions that elicit suggestions for our games.

Lesson 15: Journal Homework (Novice)

Choose three "gets" that you like. I will use some of your suggestions when I introduce the games in the performance.

RUBRIC	3 Points	2 Points	1 Point	0 Points
	Student listed three "gets."	Student listed two "gets."	Student listed one "get."	Assignment not done.

Lesson 15: Journal Homework (Advanced)

You may be introducing a game in the show and will need ideas. Pick three that you would feel comfortable using.

RUBRIC	3 Points	2 Points	1 Point	0 Points
	Student listed three "gets."	Student listed two "gets."	Student listed one "get."	Assignment not done.

Lesson 15: Video Homework

Look up the games that you played in class today. If you cannot find them, skim through more videos like those you watched for your last video assignment. Pay special attention to how games are introduced. You do not need to do any write ups on these videos.

Lesson 16: Performance

> *"The best thing about improv is that no matter how bad your show is, it's only 30 minutes, and never exists again. The worst thing is no matter how good your show is, it's only 30 minutes, and never exists again,"*
> -Mick Napier, co-founder Annoyance Theater

OVERVIEW: The final performance can be a time of anxiety for some and excitement for others. Harness that energy for a great show!

PRE-SHOW PREP
- Plan 30-60 minutes of prep with the students before the audience arrives.
- Hand out the line-ups and give students a few minutes to look them over.
- Post the line-up on the walls on either side of the "stage."
- Walk through the show introducing each game as you would for the performance.
- If you have a booth person doing sound and/or lights, involve them in this process so they are ready to start the music and/or turn off the lights when you call "Scene."
- If you have students introducing games, now is the time to fine-tune how they are introduced.
- Have game hosts practice one of their "gets" from the previous night's homework to elicit suggestions.
- Ask if there are any questions about how each game is run as you get to it.
- Do not practice the actual game at this time.
- After getting through the line-up (approximately 5-10 minutes before showtime), pull the students to another classroom or green room to warm up.
- Let the music person stay behind to start their playlist and open up the theater to arriving guests.
- In the green room, play a warm-up game or two to get the students loose.
- Right before you return to the theater, have each student pat every other student on the back saying "Got your back." This is the traditional pregame ritual for many improv troupes.

THE PERFORMANCE:
- Here is a sample script of how to run the show...
  - Have students run onto the stage and take the back line.
  - As teacher, you run out to center stage to open up the show. Music stops here.
  - *Welcome to the (Troupe Name - See Sidebar) improv class performance.*
  - Students set up for the first game. Any students not performing move to the side of the stage.
    - Example: Hi-Jacked (Any high paced game works here) - Two students set up chairs down center stage and sit in them. Other performing students line up behind the chairs.
  - *For our first pair I need two letters of the alphabet, such as M and P.*
  - Get letters for each pair (RB, LV, etc).
  - *Let us review:* Pairs take turns stepping up to the seats and saying their initials. First pair ends up in the the seats.
  - *I will go ahead and give the first pair their start. This car has just been hijacked by Rowdy Babies. This game is called Hi-jacked.*

Improv Troupe Names:
Improv troupes are known to have silly names. Sometimes these names are inside jokes, other times they are a play on words. A quick Google search will give you an idea of how ridiculous they can get. Allow your students to come up with some ideas and vote on their favorite.

- Step off to the side of stage and edit each couple with one bell ring or clap.
- After each group has gotten at least two run throughs, end the game on a big laugh with several dings of the bell.
- Booth person starts the music, flips the lights.
* Continue to run the Line-Up.
* End with a full class game (Freeze, Slide Show, etc).
* At the end have all the students stand on the back line.
* *Thank you all for joining us for our end of class performance!*
* Add positive personal observations about the work the students put in.
* *Collectively we are "The [Troupe Name] Improv Class" but individually we are…*
* Introduce the furthest student on the back line. That student should run forward and give some sort of a silly bow.
* That student introduces the person next to them, and so forth.
* Don't forget to thank the booth person.
* Booth person turns up the music and the class leaves the stage.
* At this point it is traditional in many short form shows to line up outside the theater to give high fives to audience members as they leave and thank them for coming.
* Congrats, you did it!

Appendixes

Appendix A: Troubleshooting

> *"90% of your problems can be solved by looking at your scene partner. The floor holds no answers."* -Chris Gethard, Upright Citizens Brigade

1. Some of my students will not participate in games because they are too anxious or embarrassed.

This is very common early in a class. Whenever possible, instead of doing games as a whole group, play in partners. This takes the pressure off of reluctant improvisors. As time goes on, most students will feel more comfortable participating. That being said, it is common to have some students who never warm up to scene work. This is fine. Know that they are soaking in the lessons being taught. Help them actively participate using one or more of these strategies:
- Give them scripted material.
- Make them the "Get Guru." Write up a list of "Gets" (from **Appendix C**) specific to the games that you are playing in class. Allow the student to ask for the get and choose the responses. Alternately, give them a device with http://www.can-i-get-a.com/ loaded on it and tell them what category you need a suggestion from. This job does require some instruction on choosing age/school appropriate responses.
- Ask them to be the "director," taking notes on good scene work to share with the class.
- Make them the "booth" person. Teach them to turn off lights when you call a scene. Have them create a playlist for the performance. Give instruction on choosing good songs for a show and staring the music in the middle of a song when a scene is edited.

2. I have students who are terrified about making associations under pressure.

If this happens during the lesson on Associations, take an alternative approach and play the game **Disassociation** below:

IMPROV ACTIVITY: Disassociation
- Students take turns saying a stream of words that are not related.
- If another student catches two words that can be associated, they call out "Association."
- The student shares the two words and how they are associated.
  - Example:
    - Student A: "frog, house, paper mache, scissors"
    - Student B: "Association! Paper mache and scissors are both used in art projects."
- The goal for the student saying the list of words is to TRY to say as many UNRELATED words as possible.
- The goal for the rest of the class is to find an association with their words as quickly as possible.
- Remind students that if they call out "association," they must have a good argument for the association.

If the fear of making associations comes up as your group gets into storytelling and scene work, play any game or scene with a 10 second delay. After each student says their line of dialogue, the next student must wait 10 seconds before they say their line. A similar strategy is to have students repeat what the person before them said before they say their own line.

Another option is to put more emphasis on object and environment work. Many students think they need to come up with ideas immediately. This is not the case. Some of the best improv I have seen had the improvisors take their time getting into the scene. They relied on environment and object work to fill in time.

3. I have a student who takes over every scene.

Work with your class on the concepts of Give and Take *[Video in Bonus Digital Material]* and Leaders and Followers. Here are two activities that are helpful.

IMPROV ACTIVITY: Follow the Leader:
- This game is for three students.
- Give them a suggestion for any scene.
- In this scene only one person may be the leader, making suggestions as to what happens.
- The other two students must follow everything that the leader does.
- At some point in the scene, signal to one of the other students that it is their turn to be the leader. This student leads for some time.
- Finally signal for the third player to take the lead to end the scene.
- **Game Debrief**: *What was it like to be the leader? What was it like to be the follower? Did you like or dislike not being able to add to the scene?*

IMPROV ACTIVITY: Backdrop:
- This game is similar to the Martha Game, but the focus is different.
- Divide the class into groups of 4-8 students.
- Assign each group an environment *(See Appendix C)*.
- The students must create a scene where no one is the center of attention.
- Students can become objects in the environment or characters.
- They can be silent or make noise.
- The only rule is they must not steal focus from any other student in the group.
  - Example: A Gym
    - Student A: The water cooler, gurgling whenever someone comes and fills their water bottle.
    - Student B: A body builder silently doing bicep curls.
    - Student C: The trainer giving feedback to the body builder.
    - Student D: A treadmill (sit on floor with legs stretched out and arms up).
    - Student E: Someone running on the treadmill.
- **Game Debrief:** *Was your group successful at being an ensemble with no one person taking focus? Was there ever a time when you found yourself taking focus? How did you know you were taking focus? What did you do to correct it? Could you be an object and take focus? How? Could you be a character and still be in the background? How?*

4. I have a few students who don't listen and jump right into saying what they want to say, even if it doesn't fit in the scene.

The solutions to this problem are the same as getting students out of their fear of associations. Play scenes with a 10 second delay (need to wait 10 seconds before responding) or require everyone to repeat what their scene partner said. If this continues to be a problem, let the class know that if someone does not listen in a scene, you will call "freeze." At this point you will tag in another student who will continue with the scene. This also encourages good listening skills from your audience.

5. My students tend to stay in one spot. They don't use the stage.

Play **Emotional Letters** as a warm up game to remind students that they have an entire stage to play with.

WARM-UP: Emotional Letters:
- Have your class take the stage.
- Tell them as a group they must make the letter A, with their bodies.
- Once they make an A, tell them to remember where they are located on the stage.
- Call out for them to form the letter B as a group.
- Remind them again to remember their location for this letter.
- Finally call out for them to form the letter C.
- After they are in their final position, tell the class that you will call out an emotion.
- Students act in that emotion as they move back to the location they were in the letter A.
- Once they form the A, call out another emotion for them to act out as they move to B, and then again to C.
- **Game Debrief**: *Did you stand in the same place for the entire game? How did it feel to move around the stage in emotions. When you perform on stage, you have the entire space to play with. Use it.*

Here are two more options for getting students to move in a scene.
- **The Improv Police:** Assign a non-performing student to be the police for each performer. The police possess giant balloons (imaginary or real). If the performer they are assigned to does not move within a scene, they call "Freeze" and "whomp" their performer to remind them to move.
- **Pause/Play:** Require that a scene start only with environment and object work. After a minute or two, pause the scene. Ask the students who their characters are, where they are and what they are doing. Tell them they may now start speaking. If they fall back to standing in one spot, pause the scene again and have them return to object/environment work without speaking.

6. My students get stuck fixating on one thing in a scene and the scene doesn't go anywhere.

Remind your students that all good stories have a conflict and that the conflict often gets worse and worse before the climax. Play the following game to get them thinking about heightening conflicts. (Remind them of the classic story mountain that they were taught in elementary school.)

IMPROV ACTIVITY: Moving the Conflict
- Split the class into groups of three or four, and have the groups stand on one side of the stage.
- Call out a conflict.
- The goal is to get your group across the room, as quickly as possible, with a storyline that heightens the conflict.
- They can take one step forward each time they come up with something that makes the problem worse.
- The storyline must make sense as if it were a standalone scene.
- Each group works on their own storyline.
- Allow each group to share their first step with the whole class. (Correct any group that doesn't seem to understand what it means to heighten their conflict).
- Give the instruction that at this point, each group can continue to take one step forward for each scenario that makes their problem worse.
- They shouldn't debate ideas. If someone suggests a workable idea they should "yes, and" it. Remember the goal is to get across the room quickly.
- All ideas must make sense. The teacher is the supreme judge of what makes sense.
- When the first group gets to the other end of the room, tell everyone to freeze.
- That group shares each step they took to make their conflict worse.
- If the story made sense and could work with a scene, that group is the winner.
- If it went off the rails, let the rest of the class continue.
- **Game Debrief:** *Was it difficult to come up with ideas to make the conflict worse? How well did your group work together? Did you go with the flow or was there some dissent? In improv, you don't have the luxury of discussing ideas. You have to "yes, and" the first idea that is thrown out there and go with it.*

7. Many of my student's scenes turn into chaos. Specifically, their conflicts all involve physical fights or yelling matches. How did I stop this?

This is very common, especially with younger improvisors. Focus on teaching non-argumentative conflicts. If you have not already played **Create a Conflict** (from Lesson 8), play it now. After playing **Create a Conflict**, play **Moving the Conflict** (see above). The best conflicts in improv scenes come from silly everyday situations (and misunderstandings). Hit this idea as often as possible.

8. I have students that think creating a story is hard.

Try **Automatic Story Telling** in partners. *(See Appendix G: Additional Game Descriptions).* One partner will be "in the know" that there is no real story. After each partnership has figured out their story, share them with the class. Discuss how everyone started with the same title, but came up with very different storylines. These stories were created simply by linking random questions together.

9. When I give my students a suggestion to start a scene they totally freeze up and say they can't think of anything.

Try this exercise:

- Sit everyone in a circle.
- Tell them to close their eyes for two minutes and think of nothing.
- Make some subtle noises, like a cough/sneeze/drop something.
- Ask if anyone was able to think of nothing during that two minutes.
- Ask if they heard you cough/sneeze/etc.
- If they heard that, then they obviously couldn't have thought of nothing for the whole two minutes.
- What went through their minds?
- Improv actors use whatever they see and hear in a room when they get stuck.
- Tell the class to close their eyes.
- On the count of three they should open them and call out the first object that they see.
- What kind of character would use that object?
- Create that character in your mind.
- Turn to the person next to you and have a short conversation as that character.
- Close eyes for 10 seconds, call out what noises you heard.
- How did the noise make you feel?
- Take that emotion and create a character/conflict/etc.

10. My students are a little overexcited and have no self-control.

When my classes seem to be a little out of control, I like to go back to a few centering activities. Here are a few options:
- **Zen Counting** *(See Appendix G: Additional Game Descriptions)*.
- **Pass the Squeeze**
  - Have all students stand in a circle holding hands.
  - Squeeze the hand of the person to your right.
  - When that student feels your squeeze, they squeeze the person to their right's hand and so on.
  - Students need to wait until they feel the squeeze of the person next to them.
  - Often a squeeze gets dropped.
  - Remind students that they are essentially "listening" with their hands.
  - Once the class has it down and the squeeze gets passed quickly and accurately, add another squeeze in the opposite direction.
  - Remind the class that it takes a lot of skill to be the one who gets both squeezes at the same time.
  - Are they ready to handle the responsibility? (This usually gets them into a serious competitive and focused mindset).
- **Silent and Serious**:
  - Partner students up.
  - Have them stand back to back until you give the signal.
  - On that signal, students face each other and must keep silent with a straight face.
  - If a student smiles or laughs they must sit down.
  - Walk around and call out students who don't sit down on their own.
  - Partner up the remaining students and run another round.
  - Continue until only a few students are remaining.
  - Call them out as winners.

11. My students talk over each other.

Bring a small nerf ball or something similar to class. Whoever holds the ball is the only one who is able to speak. If someone else has something to share, they must raise their hand and wait for the ball to be passed to them. No "keep aways" are allowed. If someone raises their hand, the person holding the ball must quickly finish what they are saying and relinquish the ball. If talking over each other in a scene is an issue, use the ball in the scene. It may make things a little awkward, but may also add an interesting element.

12. I find the object and environment work that my students do is very vague. How do I get them to be more specific?

Bring in a bunch of props to class (broom, phone, keyboard, guitar, etc). Pass out the props and have students play with them for a few minutes. Remove the props. Here are three possible activities to play:
- Call students up to the front of class to pantomime an activity using one of the props. The class guesses what the object was.
- Partner up students and have each student pantomime using the object. Partners give feedback to each other on their pantomimes. Allow partners to create a scene that revolves around using their objects. Give them time to practice the scenes. Finally allow them to perform for the class.
- Play Mime Whispers (see **Appendix G: Additional Game Descriptions**).

For environment work, the goal is to encourage students to think about actual locations that they know. A good exercise is to have them think about their bedroom or another place that means a lot to them. Partner students up. Have them take their partner on a tour of that place. Be specific as to where things are located. Remind them to think about how many steps it takes to get from one place to another. After they share, they should ask their partner if they can visualize the location. The partner should then be able to give another student a detailed tour of their partner's location.

A great example of good object and environment work is the following video from the UK version of Whose Line is it Anyway? (https://youtu.be/qil83OG5cUY) In this scene, Colin is at a fairgrounds and Ryan provides the sound effects. Both Colin and Ryan are inspired by each other.

If your students did not watch the How to Spot an Improvisor video from **Lesson 6: Be Honest Video Homework**, play it for them (https://youtu.be/3b1ZJBgJ5LM).

13. Our scenes are confusing because my students give too many random details or they don't share important details.

If you did not play **10 Second Fairy Tale** during *Lesson 8: Telling a Story*, play this game. It helps students identify key plot points and see that things can be pared down drastically and still make sense. When you play this, remind students of key plot points and the *Important Elements of Storytelling*. If you already played 10 Second Fairy Tale, try a few rounds of **Half Life (*see Appendix G: Additional Game Descriptions)*. Another option is to time your scenes. Allow only four minutes to get in all the *Important Elements of Storytelling*. After scenes, debrief with the class. Ask the audience to suggest ideas to pare down or expand the scenes. Allow the students to redo their scenes with the added suggestions.

14. I have a few students who try to throw funny one-liners or curve balls into our scenes and games.

Whenever this happens remind the class of the Teamwork Side Rule: Don't try to be funny alone *(See Side Bar Lesson 9)*. Going for the quick laugh throws the rest of your team under the bus. Talk about what happened to the scene after the one-liner or curve ball was thrown in. Usually the scene deflates or someone has to fix it. Debrief by asking students who were in the scene how they felt to have it thrown in that direction.

Another way to deal with this, is to show students that some of the best and most hilarious improv comes from playing a scene straight. A fabulous lesson is to share Real Actors Read Yelp Reviews, found here: https://www.youtube.com/channel/UCkk5prZRveihMbMwOm5UtSw These actors add emotion to otherwise non-humorous material and the results are hilarious. Find Yelp or other internet reviews for your students to practice and perform for the class. Tell them to use emotion to elicit laughs.

15. My students try to play scenes in character, using accents and they tend to put all their energy into the accent/character and lose the focus of the scene.

Learning to do good scene work is hard. Learning to do characters and accents is hard. Putting the two of these things together can be like rubbing your belly and patting your head at the same time. This is difficult even for some of the best improvisors. Remind your students that as they learn, they should play their characters straight. What does this mean? If you are endowed as a pirate, don't worry about speaking in the gruff accent of a pirate. Instead let your dialogue and object/environment work be inspired by pirates. Search the stage for a treasure. Make your scene partner walk the plank. If you are endowed as a criminal, attempt to steal your scene partner's wallet. Talk about your time in jail. A lawyer might be motivated to look at everything in a scene as if there will be a lawsuit. Tell students that if they are at a loss for what to do with their character, let it go and focus on telling the story and heightening the conflict to make the scene interesting. A good scene is more important that incorporating all the endowments/suggestions that are given at the beginning of a scene.

16. I have a couple students who cannot help but get physical with their scene partners. How do I get them to keep their bodies to themselves?

One way to get your students to focus on the elements of the scene work without being able to touch another player is to have them stay seated throughout the scene. Put two chairs back to back. Students talk their way through the scene and can even discuss the movements they are making, ("Take this plunger and use it.") but they are glued to their seats. By sitting back to back students are forced into listening to each other to figure out what to say next and cannot actually touch each other.

Another option is to play **Two Headed Scenes** *(see Appendix G: Additional Game Descriptions)*. Partner physical students with students who tend to avoid altercations. Remind students that they need to not only speak as one, but move as one, so this involves a lot of give and take. No big sudden movements from any one student.

A third option for involving these students in scenes where they cannot get physical with each other is Puppets (**see Appendix G: Additional Game Descriptions**). Assign the physical students to the roles of the puppets and assign non-physical students to the roles of puppeteers.

Appendix B: Handouts

Appendix B-1: Homework Handouts

Appendix B-2: Bad Stories Handout

Appendix B-3: Conflicts Handout

Appendix B-4: Two Person Scripts

Appendix B-5: Two Person Scene Rubric

Appendix B-6: Two Person Scene Grading Sheet

Appendix B-7: Group Scenes

Appendix B-1: Homework Handouts
Lesson 1: Teamwork and Trust

Lesson 1: Journal Homework

Tonight your assignment is to write about a time when you needed teamwork to complete a task. How did things work out? Did the team work well together? What went well? If it didn't go smoothly, what went wrong? Did you trust the people in your group? Why or why not?

	3 Points	2 Points	1 Point	0 Points
RUBRIC	Student discussed a teamwork situation with details about how things turned out and a reflection of what went well or wrong.	Student discussed a teamwork situation but is missing details about how things turned out or is missing the reflection of what went well or wrong.	Student discussed a teamwork situation but is missing details about how things turned out AND is missing a reflection of what went well or wrong.	Assignment not done.

Lesson 1: Video Homework

Watch the video clips that are listed below. Write a short reflection about what these clips have in common. What scene or game was your favorite? Why?

Whose Line Is It Anyway? UK: Secret - Priests in a Church
https://youtu.be/fBfLFt8l038

Improv-A-Ganza: Sound Effects - Race Care Drivers
https://youtu.be/ek79sMX235k

Whose Line Is It Anyway: Hollywood Director - Convicts Escaping a Chain Gang
https://youtu.be/XCPBPXKakOQ

	3 Points	2 Points	1 Point	0 Points
RUBRIC	Student wrote a reflection including what the clips had in common AND listed their favorite game and why they liked it.	Student wrote a reflection including what the clips had in common OR listed their favorite game and why they liked it.	Student wrote a reflection, but it is missing what the clips had in common AND/OR Student only listed their favorite game but not why they liked it.	Assignment not done.

Homework Handout
Lesson 2: Make Associations

Lesson 2: Journal Homework

For homework you will create five association chains. Grab a magazine or a book that contains a lot of pictures. Open up to a random page and write down the first object you see. Open to another page and write down the first object you see on that page. In 4-6 steps, make a chain of associations to connect the two objects. Give yourself no more that one minute to make your connection.

Example:
High chair + headphones: High chair, feeding a baby, baby screaming, trying to escape, putting on headphones.

RUBRIC	3 Points	2 Points	1 Point	0 Points
	Student wrote 5 association chains.	Student wrote 3-4 association chains.	Student wrote 1-2 association chains.	Assignment not done.

Lesson 2: Video Homework

Tonight you will watch two video clips of the game Freeze. This game is all about making new associations based on players' physical positions. While watching the videos think about associations that you would make based on some of the positions the actors are in. List three things that you would have done if you were in either of those games of Freeze. For instance, in the first video, when Wayne, Brad and Jonathan are back to back to back, I thought about a conga line. In the second video, with the downward dog position that Jeff Davis was in, I thought of a dog house. Don't overthink it. Whatever comes to your mind, use it. There is no wrong.

Improv-A-Ganza: Freeze
https://youtu.be/DZZH3RMATQY

Improv-A-Ganza: Freeze
https://youtu.be/qj__tWwUulA

RUBRIC	3 Points	2 Points	1 Point	0 Points
	Student listed three things they would have done.	Student listed two things they would have done.	Student listed one thing they would have done.	Assignment not done.

Homework Handout
Lesson 3: Yes, and

Lesson 3: Journal Homework

In creating obstacles, we had to imagine a specific environment. Tonight for homework, in your journal, write ten specific locations. For instance, not just a beach, but Point Dume State Beach. Not a park, but Ruby Carson Memorial Park. Label the top of the page LOCATIONS. We will use this list as inspiration in future classes.

	3 Points	2 Points	1 Point	0 Points
RUBRIC	Student wrote 10 detailed locations.	Student wrote a list, but it contained less than 10 locations OR the locations were not specific.	Student wrote a list containing less than 10 locations AND the locations were not specific.	Assignment not done.

Lesson 3: Video Homework

Watch the Mick Napier You Tube Video Entitled "A Place of Yes." Watch how a scene works with acceptance and how it goes nowhere when there is negation. Then write a short reflection about what you thought of the video and the two performances.

Mick Napier: A Place of Yes
https://youtu.be/mYv4vAnnuts

	3 Points	2 Points	1 Point	0 Points
RUBRIC	Student wrote a reflection that included specific references to both performances in the video.	Student wrote a reflection that included specific references to one of the performances in the video.	Student wrote a reflection but did not mention any specifics from the video.	Assignment not done.

Homework Handout
Lesson 4: Listen

Lesson 4: Journal Homework

In the warm-up we used stock characters with unique voices. For tonights homework you must come up with a list of ten different characters that an actor could use in a scene. They may be basic characters, such as a doctor or teacher or very specific characters, such as Wonder Woman or a pirate who has lost their treasure. You can use any of these characters in future classes when you need to endow another performer with a character ("You are an angry preschooler") or whenever you want to become a specific character in a scene.

	3 Points	2 Points	1 Point	0 Points
RUBRIC	Student wrote a list of 10 characters.	Student wrote a list of 5-9 characters.	Student wrote a list of 1-4 characters.	Assignment not done.

Lesson 4: Video Homework

Watch the following videos from Canadian Improv Games and One Minute Improv on listening. These videos sum up what we talked about today and give a little added information about how listening can help you in a scene. Then watch the game Two-Headed Expert from Improv-A-Ganza. This is an example of how the two-headed people work together in an actual scene. List 3 times you noticed the players listening to one another.

Canadian Improv Games: Listening
http://improv.ca/listening/

One Minute Improv: Listening
https://youtu.be/b-31atJrKdI

Improv-A-Ganza: Two Headed Expert (Organic Chemistry)
https://youtu.be/y7YS8JbbqyQ

	3 Points	2 Points	1 Point	0 Points
RUBRIC	Student wrote three examples of listening.	Student wrote two examples of listening.	Student wrote one example of listening.	Assignment not done.

Homework Handout
Lesson 5: Relate

Lesson 5: Video Homework

Tonight I want you to start with the video portion of your homework. Watch the following video of The Laff Staff performing an Armando on stage. In a typical Armando, players do not perform the stories literally, as we did in class (with the beginning, middle and end), but instead take ideas they get from relating to the story told. These ideas are turned into scenes "based" off the monologue. Name three "items" picked out from one of the monologues that were brought into the performance. These could be an emotion, a character, a location, an idea, etc.

The Laff Staff: Armando
https://youtu.be/bPqX4H3qGFw

RUBRIC	3 Points	2 Points	1 Point	0 Points
	Student wrote three items gleaned from one of the monologues.	Student wrote two items gleaned from one of the monologues.	Student wrote one item gleaned from one of the monologues.	Assignment not done.

Lesson 5: Journal Homework

Tonight for homework, I want you to go to http://www.can-i-get-a.com. Click on the location, relationship, or word button. This is going to be your suggestion. Use that word to spark a memory from your life. If you can't come up with anything, click another button until you find something that gives you an idea. Write the story in your journal. Make sure you fill in lots of details. If we were doing an Armando, this would be your "monologue."

RUBRIC	3 Points	2 Points	1 Point	0 Points
	Student wrote a detailed story based on a suggestion.	Student wrote a story but it lacked details.	Student wrote ideas, but they were not connected into a story.	Assignment not done.

Homework Handout
Lesson 6: Be Honest

Lesson 6: Journal Homework

In your journal create a character who is opposite from yourself. Draw a picture of what this character looks like. Give them a name, an age, an occupation, a family. Make it as detailed as possible (things they like, things they dislike). Make sure this is a character that you will be able to play, as we will be using these characters later in the class.

RUBRIC	3 Points	2 Points	1 Point	0 Points
	Student created a character, drew a picture of them and gave them a full backstory.	Student created a character with a basic backstory.	Student created a character without a backstory.	Assignment not done.

Lesson 6: Video Homework

Watch the following video clips and take note of the object and environment work. The first shows improvisors performing bad object work with actual props. Make a list of five mistakes to avoid with object work. The second video is a two person scene that includes good object, environment and character work. Finally, the last video is one scene from a long-form Armando where an improvisor goes through a very elaborate set of entries to get to a bomb shelter. He commits to his environment work and the audiences love it.

Chris Bresler: How to Spot an Improvisor (Safe for Work Version)
https://youtu.be/3b1ZJBgJ5LM

Improv-A-Ganza: New Choice - Nice Restaurant
https://youtu.be/DxdLiE6Eq7E

iO: The Armando Diaz Show - Jason Entry
https://youtu.be/kr5xjoOnAec

RUBRIC	3 Points	2 Points	1 Point	0 Points
	Student wrote 5 mistakes to avoid.	Student wrote 3-4 mistakes to avoid.	Student wrote 1-2 mistakes to avoid.	Assignment not done.

Homework Handout
Lesson 7: Be in the Present

Lesson 7: Journal Homework

Today we learned that scenes begin with strong initiations. These initiations are often present tense emotional statements. Tonight write a list of five powerful statements that could open a scene.

	3 Points	2 Points	1 Point	0 Points
RUBRIC	Student wrote a list of 5 strong opening statements.	Student wrote a list of less than 5 statements OR some of their statements were not strong.	Student wrote a list of less than 5 statements AND some of their statements were not strong.	Assignment not done.

Lesson 7: Video Homework

Tonight you will see why some improvisors say another rule of improv is "Make statements, not questions" As beginning improvisors we often get scared in a scene and ask our partner questions. When we do this, we force our partner to create things or worse yet, they turn the question right back on us and the scene doesn't go anywhere. Tonight's videos include one that shows questions leading a scene nowhere. The other shows how good improvisors use questions to further a scene. It also shows how hard it is to avoid statements. (Notice how many times actors get buzzed out of the game). In your journal list three examples of questions to avoid in scenes. (You will find these in the first video). Extra credit point if you come up with an example of a question that a character might use in a scene that includes information to further the scene.

The Rules of Improv: The "Questions Only" Improv Game
https://youtu.be/kH-_0sg_KMM

Whose Line Is It Anyway - Questions Only - International Flight (Starts at 50 seconds)
https://dai.ly/x55jdgt

	3 Points	2 Points	1 Point	0 Points
RUBRIC	Student wrote three examples of questions to avoid.	Student wrote two examples of questions to avoid.	Student wrote one examples of questions to avoid.	Assignment not done.

Homework Handout
Lesson 8: Tell a Story (Part I)

Lesson 8: Journal Homework

Novice
Utilizing the Story Spine, write a story including all the Important Elements of Storytelling.

Advanced
Utilizing one of the conflicts you created in Create a Conflict, write a story including all the Important Elements of Storytelling.

	3 Points	2 Points	1 Point	0 Points
RUBRIC	Student wrote a story that included all the *Important Elements of Storytelling*.	Student wrote a story that missed one *Important Element of Storytelling*.	Student wrote a story that missed more than one *Important Element of Storytelling*.	Assignment not done.

Lesson 8: Video Homework

Video Assignment: Watch the Roman Improv Games clip. In your journal, list the characters, location and conflict.

Roman Improv Games: Speak in One Voice
https://youtu.be/hoTAziyhO7s

Additional Video: If you talked about playing the game within the game with your students, assign this additional video of Keegan Michael-Key discussing setting up the rules and then playing the game within those parameters.

The Off Camera Show: Keegan-Michael Key Has the Perfect Metaphor for Improv
https://youtu.be/coZARWbdNls

	3 Points	2 Points	1 Point	0 Points
RUBRIC	Student listed the characters, location and conflict.	Student listed the two of the three required items.	Student listed one of the required items.	Assignment not done.

Homework Handout
Lesson 9: Tell a Story (Part II)

Lesson 9: Journal Homework

For your journal assignment, grab a magazine or a book with lots of pictures. Open to a random page and pick out a picture. Using that image as an inspiration, write a story including the Important Elements of Storytelling.

<u>Advanced Students:</u>
Try to challenge yourself to create a pattern and play a game with your story.

	3 Points	2 Points	1 Point	0 Points
RUBRIC	Student wrote a story that included all the *Important Elements of Storytelling*.	Student wrote a story with one missing *Important Element of Storytelling*.	Student wrote a story with more than one *Important Element of Storytelling* missing.	Assignment not done.

Lesson 9: Video Homework

Watch the TEDx improvisation scene inspired by mayonnaise and puppy. Summarize the story. Include the main characters, the beginning, the conflict, the resolution of the conflict and the ending.

<u>Advanced Group:</u>
Extra credit point if you list at least one time the improvisors played the game within the game.

The art of improvisation - Rapid Fire Theater - TEDxEdmonton
https://youtu.be/d3TsyT_EDBc

	3 Points	2 Points	1 Point	0 Points
RUBRIC	Student wrote a summary including the main characters, the beginning, the conflict, the resolution of the conflict and the ending.	Student wrote a summary but was missing 1-2 key components.	The student wrote a summary but was missing more than 2 key components.	Assignment not done.

Homework Handout
Lesson 10: Develop Relationships

Lesson 10: Journal Homework

Come up with a list of three scenarios where high and low status could be played opposite or heightened for comedic effect. Example: The class bully and the class wimp, but instead of stealing lunch money the bully gives the money to the wimp.

RUBRIC	3 Points	2 Points	1 Point	0 Points
	Student listed three scenarios.	Student listed two scenarios.	Student listed one scenario.	Assignment not done.

Lesson 10: Video Homework

Tonight you will watch one improv scene and two sketch comedy pieces. After watching the first video, list three ways the actors raised or lowered their status. Next check out the two sketch comedy pieces. Sketches are usually developed after exploring ideas through improv scenes. The following sketches have good examples of both status play and playing the game within the game. Mr Show's "24 is the Highest Number" is a fantastic example of taking a ridiculous premise and running with it for comedic affect.

Slide Quest - Status Switch
https://youtu.be/Q4TaA_2ZW6o

Mr Show with Bob and David - Season 3 Episode 7 - "24 is the Highest Number"
https://youtu.be/RkP_OGDCLY0 (Full episode available on Amazon Prime. Sketch starts at 11:30)

Key and Peele - Substitute Teacher
https://youtu.be/Dd7FixvoKBw

RUBRIC	3 Points	2 Points	1 Point	0 Points
	Student listed 3 ways the players raised or lowered their status.	Student listed 2 ways the players raised or lowered their status.	Student listed 1 way the players raised or lowered their status.	Assignment not done.

Teaching Improv - A Beat by Beat Book

Homework Handout
Lesson 11: Two Person Scenes (Part I)

Lesson 11: Journal Homework

Reflect upon your script and performance from today's lesson. What element was the easiest to come up with? Why? What was the hardest to come up with? Why? What do you feel your strengths are in improv? What areas do you want to improve upon?

RUBRIC	3 Points	2 Points	1 Point	0 Points
	Student wrote a reflection that included the easy and hard elements, strengths AND areas of improvement.	Student wrote a reflection that was missing one of the elements.	Student wrote a reflection that was missing more than one of the elements.	Assignment not done.

Lesson 11: Video Homework

Watch the following video clips of short form improv games. We will play versions of these in upcoming classes. Choose your favorite of the games and write at least three reasons why you liked it. Was it the format of the game? An actor's performance or character you to related to? The heightening of a pattern? Be specific as to why you enjoyed the scene.

Improv-A-Ganza: New Choice - Acrobatics (start the video at 1:45)
https://youtu.be/Mwra1FeNrS4

Four Square: The Second City Improv
https://youtu.be/hAmHgF21U-k

Jackson Adventure Video: The Laff Staff - Hijacked
https://youtu.be/wW8pkB93-dc

RUBRIC	3 Points	2 Points	1 Point	0 Points
	Student listed their favorite game and 3 specific reasons why they liked it.	Student listed their favorite game and 2 specific reasons why they liked it.	Student listed their favorite game and 1 specific reasons why they liked it OR they listed 2-3 reasons but the reasons were not specific.	Assignment not done.

Homework Handout
Lesson 12: Two Person Scenes (Part II)

Lesson 12: Journal Homework

Tonight write a short reflection about your biggest successes in today's scenes and mention at least one thing you struggled with. What could you practice to work on that struggle?

	3 Points	2 Points	1 Point	0 Points
RUBRIC	Student wrote a reflection including successes and one area of struggle. They listed something they could work on.	Student wrote a reflection including successes and at least one thing they struggled with but did not come up with something to practice.	Student wrote a reflection including successes OR one thing they struggled with AND did not come up with something to practice.	Assignment not done.

Lesson 12: Video Homework

Video Homework: Tonight's video homework gives you a sneak peak at how scenes with more than two players work. You have already seen the Armando. This time, I want you to focus on the dynamics on stage when there are more than two performers in a scene. Skip past the monologues to the scenes. Write three observations you made about the performances in the Armando or the Whose Line Is It Anyway group scenes.

Laff Staff: Armando
https://youtu.be/bPqX4H3qGFw?t=138

Whose Line is it Anyway: Old Job, New Job - Undertake Used to be a Used Car Salesman
https://youtu.be/l4fwDNWuUto

Whose Line is it Anyway: Superheroes - There's a Dead Possum in his Parking Spot (start at 0:45)
https://bit.ly/2tUtQvo

	3 Points	2 Points	1 Point	0 Points
RUBRIC	Listed three observations.	Listed two observations.	Listed one observation.	Assignment not done.

Teaching Improv - A Beat by Beat Book

Homework Handout
Lesson 13: Group Scenes

Lesson 13: Journal Homework

Directions: Attached to this handout is a list of all the games we have played in class. Circle your favorite warm-up game. Rate every other game on a scale of 1-3. This is how games for the performance will be chosen.
1 = Disliked it
2 = Liked It
3 = Loved It.

RUBRIC	3 Points	2 Points	1 Point	0 Points
	Rated every game and circled the games they wanted to play.	Rated most games and circled the games they wanted to play.	Rated some games and/or didn't circle games they wanted to play.	Assignment not done.

Lesson 13: Video Homework

Watch the following clips of guessing games to prepare for the next class. List three things you noticed the endowed performers do that made it possible for the guessing player to guess.

Laughing Stock Improv: Late for Work (skip to 15:08)
https://youtu.be/MpH5R-7a4i0?t=906

Whose Line Is It Anyway: Party Quirks (Skip to 15:32 - 18:15)
https://bit.ly/2UNzDhs

RUBRIC	3 Points	2 Points	1 Point	0 Points
	Listed three things.	Listed two things.	Listed one thing.	Assignment not done.

Teaching Improv - A Beat by Beat Book

Homework Handout
Lesson 14: Guessing Games

Lesson 14: Journal/Video Homework

Your homework tonight is to watch more improv. Search youtube.com for Improv-A-Ganza, Whose Line Is It Anyway, and Laughing Stock TV for ideas of professional short form improv games and shows. If you search high school improv you will find examples of students your age performing. Write a short reflection about one of the videos that you watched. Include the URL, name of video, what you liked or didn't like about the game/performance.

	3 Points	2 Points	1 Point	0 Points
RUBRIC	Student wrote a short reflection including the URL, name of video and an explanation of what they liked or didn't like.	Student wrote a short reflection that was missing the URL, name of video OR an explanation of what they liked or didn't like.	Student wrote a short reflection that was missing two of the three required elements.	Assignment not done.

Homework Handout
Lesson 15: Performance and Creating a Line-Up

Lesson 15: Journal Homework (Novice)

Choose three "gets" that you like. I will use some of your suggestions when I introduce the games in the performance.

RUBRIC	3 Points	2 Points	1 Point	0 Points
	Student listed three "gets."	Student listed two "gets."	Student listed one "get."	Assignment not done.

Lesson 15: Video Homework

Look up the games that you played in class today. If you cannot find them, skim through more videos like those you watched for your last video assignment. Pay special attention to how games are introduced. You do not need to do any write ups on these videos.

Lesson 15: Journal Homework (Advanced)

You may be introducing a game in the show and will need ideas. Pick three that you would feel comfortable using.

RUBRIC	3 Points	2 Points	1 Point	0 Points
	Student listed three "gets."	Student listed two "gets."	Student listed one "get."	Assignment not done.

Lesson 15: Video Homework

Look up the games that you played in class today. If you cannot find them, skim through more videos like those you watched for your last video assignment. Pay special attention to how games are introduced. You do not need to do any write ups on these videos.

Appendix B-2: Bad Stories

STORY 1: Francesco and the Rent Money

Once upon a time there was a boy named Francesco. Francesco lived in a small apartment in the city. One day he was finishing his breakfast when there was a knock at the door. It was his landlord Mr. Smith. Mr. Smith told Francesco that his rent was past due and that if he didn't pay by the next day he would be evicted. Francesco was terrified. He had blown away the money at the casino the night before. He had no idea how he could come up with another $500 in one day. He felt relief as he handed the money to Mr. Smith and vowed never to gamble again.

STORY 2: Go to Bed

It was a dark and stormy night. Someone was putting their kid to bed. Every time they left the room, the kid would sneak out and run back downstairs into the living room. On the third time that the kid snuck out of the room, the person was furious. "Go to bed!" they screamed as they chased the kid up the stairs. This time they knew what to do. They pulled out their drill and the lock that they had been meaning to put on the door for months. Tonight was the night. They screwed the lock on the door, told the kid goodnight and slid the lock tight after closing the door. Five minutes later, the kid tried to open the door to no avail. The kid screamed as loud as they could for five minutes and then passed out on the floor. The person quietly slid open the lock, opened the door enough to sneak in and carried the kid back their bed.

STORY 3: Martha and George and the Hot Date

Every Friday, Martha and George had a hot date. For 50 years of marriage they went to their favorite spot and ate dinner. This Friday was different. They showed up and the door was locked. How could this be? For 50 years they had come to this place and now, out of nowhere it was closed. George was furious, but Martha, always the calm one in the relationship, told her beloved husband that maybe after 50 years it was time for a change. They walked down the street to another place and walked in the door. Now was the time for a new tradition to begin.

STORY 4: Jeff and the Big Game

Jeff walked into the school gym filled with anxiety. He hadn't played a game since he had blown his knee. Would he be back to his star status? Could he lead his team to another state championship? He walked up to Mr. Salerno and said, "I'm ready to play coach." The coach was unsure if Jeff was ready to play, but their team was down 6 points and there was only 3 minutes left in the game. If anyone could bring the morale up, and lead this team to victory, it was Jeff. "OK kid," he said. "Get on the court." Jeff ran onto the court.

STORY 5: The Playground

Sylvia and Ivan loved to go to the playground together. The two siblings were two years apart and the best of friends. When they got to the park they threw off their jackets and immediately ran to the see-saw and hopped on. It was their favorite thing to do. They bobbed up and down for what seemed like an eternity. The sun started to go down and they knew that their mom would be wondering where they were. They gathered their jackets and headed home.

STORY 6: Maria Goes to the Circus

Maria was in tears and on the verge of a temper tantrum. This was her reward for filling in her entire sticker chart for good behavior. It wasn't fair that her mother lost the tickets. She deserved to go to the circus. She worked hard. Finally, as she looked through the last kitchen drawer, underneath the take out menus, Maria's mother screamed, "I found them!" Crisis averted. Maria would get to see the clowns, elephants and trapeze artists after all.

Appendix B-3: Conflicts Handout

Instructions: Read the Popular Examples of Conflicts from movies, tv and literature. Next think about how these conflicts play out in real life. Add at least two Everyday Examples for each conflict.

Man Vs. Self

Popular Examples

- The Grinch battles with the idea of bringing back the toys.
- Pinocchio wants to be a real boy.
- *Hunger Games*: Katniss deciding who she is in love with.
- *Harry Potter*: Hallows or Horcruxes?
- *Hamlet*: "To be or not to be?"

Everyday Examples

- Trying to decide who to ask to prom.
-
-
-

Man Vs. Man

Popular Examples

- Rocky verus Apollo
- Luke Skywalker versus Darth Vader
- Batman versus Joker
- Harry Potter versus Voldermort

Everyday Examples

- My little sister reads my journal.
-
-
-

Man Vs. Society

Popular Examples

- The Grinch against the Whos
- *Hunger Games:* Katniss against the Capital

Everyday Examples

- I don't want to like Taylor Swift (or insert current pop star).
-
-
-

Teaching Improv - A Beat by Beat Book

Man Vs. Nature

Popular Examples

- *Wild:* Cheryl versus the elements on the Pacific Crest Trail; blisters, weather, etc
- *Hatchet:* Brian versus the elements post plane crash; animal attacks, tornado, finding food
- *Perfect Storm:* A crew on a fishing boat stuck in the midst of the worst storm in modern times.

Everyday Examples

- We didn't dress warmly enough for sitting through this baseball game with extra innings.
-
-
-

Man Vs. Technology

Popular Examples

- *Terminator and Westworld:* Man versus Robots
- *The Matrix:* Machines put humans into a simulated reality. Neo and others wake up and rebel.
- *Frankenstein:* Man created through science becomes a monster.

Everyday Examples

- My dad has no idea how to use his smart phone.
-
-
-

Man Vs. Fates/Gods/Supernatural

Popular Examples

- Harry Potter versus the prophecy
- *Lord of the Rings:* Frodo struggles against the eye of Mordor to follow his destiny and destroy the ring.
- *The Shining:* All the characters versus the hotel which is haunted
- Any zombie movie

Everyday Examples

- The ghost haunting my house is not scary at all, in fact, he's boring.
-
-
-

Appendix B-4: Two Person Scripts

> **TWO-PERSON SCENE 1: Good Two Person Scene Script**
>
> **MOM:** *(Hold a plate and fork. Chew and swallow a piece of cake).* Matilda, this is the most delicious cake you've ever baked!
>
> **MATILDA:** Mom, I'm so glad you like it. I'm really scared that I'm not going to win the baking battle.
>
> **MOM:** Oh, I don't think you have a chance to win the baking battle. This cake doesn't taste *that* good, but it is *way* better than the last two cakes you baked. Those were totally inedible.
>
> **MATILDA:** *(Take cake plate from mom. Scrape the cake in the garbage and start washing the dish).* You are the worst mom ever! You don't support me in anything I do.
>
> **MOM:** Not true honey. *(Walk over, take the plate from Matilda and start drying it).* I supported you when you wanted to be a ballerina. *(Continue to wash the dishes).*
>
> **MATILDA:** You told everyone we knew not to go to the recital because it was going to be terrible.
>
> **MOM:** Well sure, but I showed up to support you.

Discussion Notes:
- Strong Initiation: We know what the character is doing and we know the scene is going to involve cake (though as we see the scene goes beyond the cake). Matilda's mom is already in the middle of eating the cake.
- Location: Kitchen, demonstrated through eating and then later through washing dishes
- Relationship: Mother/Daughter
- Conflict: Matilda doesn't feel her mom supports her.
- Playing the Game within the Game: The pattern that is set is the mom saying she showed up for her daughter, while the daughter points out how she wasn't supportive. The pattern could be heightened with the mother pointing out various ways she was supportive and the daughter explaining how she was not supportive at all. i.e. Mom: "I signed you up for band lessons." Matilda: "I wanted to play the saxophone and you got me a kazoo!"

TWO-PERSON SCENE 2: Missing: Strong Initiation That Starts in the Middle of the Action

(Both characters should be sitting on the floor doing nothing).

CHARLIE: Nice day.

BOB: Yes, it is pretty.

CHARLIE: I love being on the river.

BOB: Charlie, this ain't gonna work. *(Pantomime reeling in a fishing line with no fish. Continue unsuccessfully fishing for the next few lines).*

CHARLIE: It ain't my fault you forgot to pack the worms, Bob. *(Pantomime rowing a boat through the end of the scene).*

BOB: Dad told me that you packed the worms and I was supposed to bring the poles.

CHARLIE: Well dad told me that I was supposed to bring the poles and YOU were going to pack the worms. *(Put down fishing pole).*

BOB: But you DIDN'T pack the poles, I did.

CHARLIE: I just thought you were being an overachiever.

BOB: This is pointless. *(Put down fishing pole).* Hand me a sandwich.

CHARLIE: Oh I'm hungry too. Please tell me you made peanut butter and jelly.

BOB: You were supposed to pack the worms AND the lunch, Charlie.

CHARLIE: No, I was supposed to pack the poles and load the boat.

BOB: But I loaded the boat AND packed the poles!

CHARLIE: I just thought you were being an overachiever.

Discussion Notes:
- **Missing: Strong Initiation.** Starting with the line "nice day" gives us very little to go on. We don't know who, where or what. If they had started rowing the boat from the first line of the scene, that environment work would have made for a strong initiation.
- <u>Location</u>: on a row boat in the river
- <u>Relationship</u>: brothers
- <u>Conflict</u>: Charlie didn't do anything he was supposed to, so they are missing half of what they need.
- <u>Playing the Game Within the Game:</u> The pattern set is miscommunication as to who was supposed to take care of what. Bob took care of everything that Charlie thought he was supposed to do, so Charlie thought that Bob was being an overachiever. The pattern could be heightened by the brothers missing more and more important items.
  - Example:
    - BOB: Ouch! I saw the first aid kit in your hands at home. Please tell me you put the first aid kit it in boat.
    - CHARLIE: I did have it in my hand. But I figured you were the one allergic to bees so there would be no way you would forget to pack it. I left it on the counter for you.

TWO-PERSON SCENE 3: Missing: Location

(Both players move about the stage during the scene but should not be specific as to where they are).

MANUEL: Jaida, I don't know why you keep insisting that crocodiles are more interesting than alligators.

JAIDA: Well Manuel, it is just a fact. The television show was not called Alligator Hunter. Why? Because Crocodile Hunter is much better.

MANUEL: I don't think it sounds any better that way, sweetheart.

JAIDA: Oh it does. In fact, crocodile sounds better before most words. The movie was called Crocodile Dundee for a reason.

MANUEL: Yes, because the guy was in Australia with a bunch of crocodiles. In fact, the Crocodile Hunter was Australian too. Maybe if these shows were based in Florida they would be alligator shows.

JAIDA: Well we all know that Australian accents are far more interesting than Floridian accents, so you are just helping me make my point, dear.

Discussion Notes:
- **Missing: Location:** This scene works, but it would be better if we knew where this couple was arguing. Adding specific "environment work" to a scene adds to the scene's complexity.
- Strong Initiation: Manuel makes a bold statement about the fight they are in the middle of.
- Relationship: They are a couple - "dear" "sweetheart"
- Conflict: One thinks crocodiles are more interesting than alligators and the other doesn't agree. Conflicts can be silly.
- Playing the Game Within the Game: The argument here would get old if a new pattern wasn't formed. Jaida could introduce another pair of items to compare, saying one is more interesting than the other.
  - Example:
    - JAIDA: Speaking of Florida, you know something else that is interesting? Flamingos.
    - MANUELI: I suppose.
    - JAIDA: It's a fact that flamingos are more interesting than ostriches.

TWO-PERSON SCENE 4: Missing: Relationship

NAOMI: I can't believe how huge this big top is! *(Look around in awe).*

LEVI: This IS the Greatest Show on Earth!

NAOMI: Come on. Let's sneak behind the curtains.

LEVI: I don't think we are supposed to go back there. We could get into trouble.

NAOMI: Who cares. We might get a chance to see a clown or even walk on the tightrope.

LEVI: Whoa whoa whoa…trying to see a clown is one thing, but walking on the tightrope? That is just stupid.

Discussion Notes:
- **Missing: Relationship.** We are unclear of how Levi and Naomi know each other. Adding in a line, such as "Mom will be mad" or "We need to stay with our class" gives us a point of connection. (There is a status play going on here that could be played further. Naomi could take on more control with Levi reluctantly and nervously following her).
- <u>Location</u>: The circus
- <u>Strong Initiation</u>: This initiation lets us know the location. They are already walking around the tent.
- <u>Conflict</u>: Naomi wants to break the rules and Levi is a rule follower.
- <u>Playing the Game Within the Game</u>: The pattern that is set is Naomi wants to break rules. She has already gone to one heightened idea with walking the tightrope. She could continue this pattern and keep the scene in the present by interacting with increasingly more dangerous elements of the circus.
- Example:
  - NAOMI: Come on. The lion cage is right over here.

TWO-PERSON SCENE 5: Missing: Conflict

BAILEY: *(Pantomime putting ornaments on a tree)*. Tiana, I can't believe we finally get to decorate the office Christmas tree.

TIANA: *(Join in the decoration)*. I know Bailey. It seems like every year they pick someone else.

BAILEY: Finally, the accountants get a turn.

TIANA: We are going to make this the best decorated tree the office has ever seen.

BAILEY: Yes, I am going to put tinsel all over this thing.

TIANA: I am going to make sure that the star is the biggest star ever.

BAILEY: I might even put candy canes on it.

Discussion Notes:
- **Missing: Conflict.** There are lots of "yes, and"s in this scene, but the scene is going nowhere since there is only agreement.
- Strong Initiation: Decorating the tree is a strong action that is in process as the scene starts. We know what they are doing and that Bailey is excited about it.
- Relationship: Co-workers
- Location: Office
- Playing the Game Within the Game: Adding a conflict will allow for a game to be discovered. Early on Bailey mentions that the accountants finally get their turn. Why haven't they been allowed to decorate the tree in the past? Perhaps they are clumsy and break all the ornaments. Another option would be that they are terrible at decorating.
  - Example:
    - TIANA: Whoa, whoa, the only thing that should be on a Christmas tree is a huge star and eleven pieces of tinsel.
    - BAILEY: Eleven pieces of tinsel? This tree needs fourteen pieces of tinsel.

Appendix B-5: Two Person Scene Rubric

	3 Points	2 Points	1 Point
Location	Student utilized environment work and dialogue to demonstrate a specific location.	Student utilized some environment work and dialogue to demonstrate a non-specific location.	Location was unclear from the performance.
Character	Student clearly portrayed who their character was and what their motivation was in the scene.	Student portrayed a character but it was not always clear who they were and/or it was not always clear what their motivation was.	Student did not portray a character and did not show motivation.
Relationship	Student demonstrated a relationship with details.	Student demonstrated a relationship but it was not detailed.	Student did not have a relationship to the other student in the scene.
Strong Initiation	Scene began with a strong initiation that was in the middle of the action.	Scene began with a strong initiation but was not in the middle of the action OR the scene began in the middle of the action, but their initiation was not strong.	Scene did not have a strong initiation and did not begin in the middle of the action.
Conflict	Scene had a clear and detailed conflict.	Scene had a conflict but it got lost along the way.	Scene did not have a conflict.
Game Within the Game	Student utilized a pattern to heighten the conflict OR played off of the high/low status of their characters.	Student attempted to play the game within the game, but it fell short.	Student did not attempt to play the game within the game.

Appendix B-6: Two Person Scene Grading Sheet

Student Name:	Location	Character	Relationship	Strong Initiation	Conflict	Game Within the Game

Appendix B-7: Group Scenes

GROUP SCENE 1

BERNARD: *(Kneeling on ground picking up shards of glass).* You shouldn't have thrown the ball in the house. Mom is going to kill us.

SHARON: *(Helping pick up the glass).* This was grandma's vase.

BERNARD: You think I don't know that?! She cries every time she walks past it.

MOM: *(Enter scene).*

(Sharon and Bernard try to hide the broken vase with their bodies).

MOM: Kids, it's time to go.

GROUP SCENE 2

[Cut up the slips of dialogue and hand out to seven students. Student A and B start the scene and stay throughout. Other students enter after the previous student leaves].

STUDENT A: Stand next to Student B and stare at a painting on the wall (located downstage). Improvise dialogue about how confusing the painting is. As each new student enters, react honestly, in your character, to their statements.

STUDENT B: Stand next to Student A and stare at a painting on the wall (located downstage). Improvise dialogue about how stupid the painting is and that it makes no sense. As each new student enters, react honestly, in your character, to their statements.

STUDENT C: Enter the scene after a few lines of Student A and Student B dialogue. Say the following line: "Hey guys, what's happening?" Freeze. Wait for teacher to debrief this line, then exit the scene.

STUDENT D: Enter scene after Student C exits the scene. Look at painting on the wall. Name the piece of artwork and make a comment about how powerful it is. Exit.

STUDENT E: Enter scene after Student D leaves. Look at painting on the wall. Name the painter and say how brilliant they are. Exit.

STUDENT F: Enter scene after Student E leaves. Look at painting on the wall. Improvise a line about the painting changing your life. Exit.

STUDENT G: Enter scene after Student F leaves. Look at painting on the wall. Improvise a line about how ridiculously stupid the painting is. Exit.

GROUP SCENE 3

(Mike and Chris are on one side of the stage. Becky and Three Back-Up Girls are clumped on the other side).

MIKE: I think Becky is the one. I might ask her to the Homecoming dance.

CHRIS: You should do it soon man. You might miss your chance.

MIKE: I just wish she wasn't always surrounded by that group of giddy girls. *(Walk over to Becky and the girls).* Hey Becky.

(Girls giggle behind Becky).

BECKY: Hey Mike. *(Turn to the Back-Up Girls and giggle).*

MIKE: The Homecoming dance is coming up. *(Girls giggle).* I was wondering if, um, maybe, um, you might want to go with me.

BECKY: *(Turn to Back-Up Girls and giggle).* Gee Mike, I have three offers on the table. I'm weighing my options. Brian said that he would get me a corsage. Nick told me that he would take me to dinner at Chili's. Dante offered up a limo ride.

MIKE: *(Turn to Chris).* Dude, I don't have money for a limo!

CHRIS: Tell her you'll rent a Hummer stretch limo with a hot tub. What is she going to do when you show up with your dad in his Ford Escort?

Appendix C: Lists

OBJECTS

- Bridge
- Taco
- Washing Machine
- Dish Washer
- Sailboat
- Dog House
- TV Set
- Lamp
- Toaster
- Bed
- Rug
- Orange
- Flower
- Hot Tub
- Door
- Tin Can
- Banana
- Bowl of Mashed Potatoes
- Bowling Ball
- Scissors
- Basket of Pencils
- Pinwheel
- Peppers
- Bowler Hat
- Flying Saucer
- Fancy Car
- Wing Nut
- Clock
- Icicle
- Bicycle/Unicycle/Tricycle
- Popcycle
- Blocks
- Book
- Ferris Wheel
- Truck/Car/Motorcycle
- T-Shirt/Jeans/Dress/Skirt
- Refrigerator
- Oven
- Sink
- Table
- Chair
- Kindle
- iPad
- Board Game
- Guitar
- Magazine
- Whisk
- Fur Coat
- X-Ray
- Stuffed Animal
- Cowboy Boot
- Cape

LOCATIONS

- Beach
- Mall
- Classroom
- Office
- Gym
- Cave
- Haunted House
- Bedroom
- Attic
- Kitchen
- Bathroom
- Elevator
- Playground
- Bus Stop
- Doctor's Office
- Grocery Store
- Gas Station
- Bank
- Ice Cream Shop
- Clothing Store
- County Fair
- Riding Arena
- Zoo
- School
- Day Care Center
- Coffee Shop
- Library
- Book Store
- Construction Site
- Wood Shop
- Airport
- Train Station
- Restaurant
- Rec Center
- Theater
- Wilderness
- Forest
- Desert
- Garbage Dump
- Hotel

CHARACTERS

- Used Car Salesman
- Pilot
- Astronaut
- Zombie
- Cheerleader
- Nerd
- Anyone with a foreign accent
- Doctor
- Nurse
- Cowboy/girl
- Dancer
- Pirate
- Darth Vadar
- 5 Year Old
- Business Person
- Clown
- 80 Year Old
- Teacher
- Zoo Keeper
- Boxer
- Baker
- Auctioneer
- Butcher
- Chef
- Conductor
- Trapeze Artist
- Firefighter
- Police Officer
- Hunter
- Judge
- Model
- Shepard
- Plumber
- Stunt Man
- Referee
- Sports Announcer
- Skier/Snowboarder
- Ice Dancer
- Surfer

ACTIONS

- Brushing teeth
- Taking a shower
- Riding a motorcycle
- Making Cotton Candy
- Driving a car
- Blowing bubbles
- Building a sand castle
- Painting a fence
- Tying a shoe
- Learning a sport
- Cooking breakfast
- Hailing a taxi
- Typing
- Fishing
- Making a fire
- Getting dressed
- Taking a test
- Changing oil on a car
- Cleaning the windshield
- Shelving books
- Hammering a nail
- Cutting down a tree
- Sewing
- Playing dress-up

RELATIONSHIPS

- Parent and Child
- Teacher and Student
- Boss and Employee
- Coworkers
- Movie Star and Fan
- Athlete and Coach
- Married couple
- Bank Robber and Bank Teller
- Child and Dog
- Cat and Mouse
- Siblings
- Two hostages stuck together
- Best friends
- Two birds in flight
- Genie and Master
- Superhero and Nemesis
- Child and Invisible Friend
- Puppet and Puppeteer
- Celebrity and Obsessed fan
- Ghostbuster and Ghost
- Predator and Prey
- Limo Driver and Passenger
- Police officer and Inmate
- Dentist and Patient
- President and Vice President
- Politician and Campaign Manager
- Mad Scientist and Assistant
- Neighbors
- Competitors on a game show
- Gambler and Card Dealer
- Army Private and Lieutenant
- Chef and Server

EMOTIONS

- Friendly
- Angry
- Sad
- Embarrassed
- Frustrated
- Annoyed
- Eager
- Shy
- Nervous
- Confident
- Proud
- Fascinated
- Excited
- Energetic
- Surprised
- Grateful
- Touched
- Hopeful
- Happy
- Peaceful
- Passionate
- Anxious
- Exhausted
- Disappointed

TV/FILM STYLES

- Soap opera
- Kung fu
- Drama
- Comedy
- Shakespeare
- Courtroom Drama
- Foreign film
- Horror
- Opera
- Musical
- Science Fiction
- Documentary
- Western
- News Report
- Mystery
- Romance
- Action
- Super Hero
- Suspence
- Animal Planet
- Game Show
- Reality
- Home Improvement
- Mockumentary

OPENING LINES OF DIALOGUE/LINES FOR SENTENCES

(If you use these lines for the game Sentences, cross off any names that identify a character from the scene. i.e. Mom, Andrew).

- Mom, I need you to braid my hair.
- I am so sick sick of these Valentine's Day cards being so cheesy.
- I think we have a failure of communication here.
- Mrs. Sanchez's posole always makes me cry.
- I'll give you a tater tot if you say that word again.
- That must be the new dance they are doing.
- Your mom's not going to be home for at least another hour.
- Andrew, did you really eat all of that?
- I thought the directions said it was water-soluble.
- Ready, steady, go.
- This shampoo smells like pond scum.
- Well, heck I dropped my potato chip.
- Now I'm never going to learn to drive a car!
- When life gives you lemons…
- My mom has a poodle.
- You have an insane number of hairspray cans in here.
- I didn't even like it!
- I lost my pet lizard.
- They call me Becca now, but everyone used to call me Bucktooth B.
- At least you tried.
- This is the worst thing that has ever happened to me.
- You're crazy.
- This sandwich tastes like heaven.
- Can you just NOT?
- You ate my cheese!
- Wow, that was stupid.
- Fairies don't ever keep secrets.

LIST OF QUESTIONS TO GET SUGGESTIONS AKA "GETS"

- I need the name of a sport.
- What is something that rolls?
- What is something that flies?
- What is something that is green?
- I need the name of a city.
- What is an emotion?
- What is a musical instrument that I could have played in high school band?
- What is the name of a movie that has never been made?
- What is a location you would not want to go on spring break?
- I need the name of an occupation.
- What would be a great place/terrible place to go on a date?
- What is a style of music?
- What is something I might find in my junk drawer?
- What is the dumbest way you ever injured yourself?
- What is something that you wish you could buy online that you cannot?
- What is a problem that happens in a relationship?
- I cleaned my couch the other day and found what in the cushions?
- Name an item of clothing that you might wear in the summer/winter?
- What is an animal that you would not want to go hunting for?
- What is the name of the newest Muppet?
- What was your favorite board game when you were a kid?
- What is the newest flavor of Ben and Jerry's ice cream?
- Name a superpower that wouldn't be very helpful.
- What is the dumbest documentary subject that you can think of?
- Name a period of history.
- What is a location that would fit on this stage?
- What is a holiday that most people don't think of?
- If your house was on fire, what object would you save first?
- What animal would make a terrible pet?
- What is a room you would find in a mansion but not in a small home?
- What is your favorite cereal?
- What was the name of your favorite stuffy as a child?
- What is the strangest word you have ever heard of?
- What is the name of an illness that you got as a kid?
- What is your favorite color name from a box of crayons?
- Name a flavor of potato chips that should never be made.
- What is your favorite breakfast cereal name?
- What did your mom pack in your lunch when you were in 1st grade?
- Name a location you would not mind being lost in?
- Name a location you would never want to get lost in?
- What was the best birthday gift you ever got?
- What was the worst birthday gift you ever got?
- What was your favorite children's book growing up?
- If a goose didn't lay an egg, what would it lay?
- What is a college major that would make your parents proud? furious?

Appendix D: Sample Line-Ups

Sample Line-Up #1: Novice
- Young, immature or haven't had enough practice to hold up a two person scene.
- Involve these students in simple and low risk group games, including:
  - 3 Some
  - Great Machine
  - Translate Gibberish
  - 10 Second Object
  - Complementing Actions Game
  - Rumors
  - Yes, Let's
  - Conducted Story
  - Yes, and
  - Luckily Unluckily
  - Translate Gibberish
  - The Oracle
  - Adverbilies
  - Martha Game (without adding in opposite characters)
  - Ten Second Fairy Tale (Perform the ones they did in class).
  - Slide Show (Teacher runs the slideshow. Assign 4-6 students per slide, run enough slides that students perform in three slides).

30-40 Minute Performance

NOVICE	10 Second Object	The Oracle (2 rounds)	Martha Game	Conducted Story	Slide Show
Student A	X	X	X		X
Student B	X	X	X		X
Student C	X	X	X		X
Student D	X	X	X		X
Student E*	X		X	X	X
Student F	X		X	X	X
Student G	X		X	X	X
Student H	X		X	X	X
Student I	X		X	X	X
Student J	X		X	X	X

Teaching Improv - A Beat by Beat Book

Sample Line-Up #2: Intermediate
- Have a solid understanding of the rules of improv.
- Feel comfortable adding to a story, but are not strong enough to hold up a two person scene.
- Suggested games:
  - Rumors
  - Madison Avenue
  - Hi-Jacked
  - Two Headed Interview
  - Five Word Group Story
  - Slide Show (let strong improvisors tell the story, run two slide shows on the stage at the same time to get more kids involved)
  - String of Pearls
  - MacGyver
  - Superheroes
  - Late for Class
  - Martha Game (with someone coming in as the opposite character)

30-40 Minute Performance

Intermediate	Hi-Jacked	String of Pearls	MacGyver	Superheroes	Late for Class	Slide Show
Student A	X	X		X		PRESENTER
Student B	X	X		INTRO	X	X
Student C	X	X		X	INTRO	X
Student D	X	X			X	X
Student E	X	X		X		INTRO and X
Student F	X	X			X	PRESENTER
Student G	X	X	INTRO	X		X
Student H	X	INTRO	X		GUESSER	X
Student I *	X and INTRO		X			X and OUTRO
Student J	X		X		BOSS	X

* Student I is listed as OUTRO. The OUTRO thanks everyone for coming to the show.

Teaching Improv - A Beat by Beat Book   **111**

Sample Line-Up #3: Advanced
- Have a solid understanding of the rules of improv AND are comfortable in two person scenes.
- Suggested games:
  - Sentences
  - New Choice
  - Ping Pong
  - The Onion
  - Musical Chairs
  - Forward Reverse
  - Half Life
  - Four Square
  - Three Letter Acronym
  - Sound Effects
  - Alphabet
  - Zone-Ra
  - Puppets
  - Two Headed Scene
  - Old Job, New Job
  - Party Quirks
  - Interrogators
  - Freeze

40-60 Minute Performance

	Hi-Jacked	New Choice	The Onion	Party Quirks	Conducted Story	Four Square	Freeze
Student A	X and INTRO	X			X		X
Student B	X		X	X			X
Student C	X	X		X	CONDUCTOR & INTRO		X
Student D	X	INTRO	X			X	X
Student E	X		INTRO	GUESSER	X		X
Student F	X		X	INTRO		X	X
Student G	X			X	X	INTRO	X
Student H	X		X			X	X
Student I	X			X	X		INTRO AND X
Student J	X		X			X	X AND OUTRO

Appendix E: Final Performance Rubric

	3 Points	2 Points	1 Point	0 Points
Teamwork	Student consistently worked with their scene partners.	Student occasionally worked with their scene partners.	Students rarely worked with their scene partners.	Students did not work with their scene partners.
Statements and Associations	Student consistently made strong statements and used associations to come up with dialogue.	Student occasionally made strong statements and/or occasionally used associations to come up with dialogue.	Student did not make strong statements OR didn't use use associations to come up with dialogue.	Student did not make strong statements and did not use associations to come up with dialogue.
Yes, and	Student accepted all offers given to them and added to them.	Students accepted all offers given to them, but did not add to them.	Student denied at least one offer.	Student denied all offers.
Listen	Student consistently listened to their scene partners.	Student occasionally listened to their scene partners.	Student rarely listened to their scene partners.	Student never listened to their scene partners.
Relate	Student consistently related to their scene partners.	Student occasionally related to their scene partners.	Student rarely related to their scene partners.	Student never related to their scene partners.
Be Honest	Student consistently played their character and environment honestly in their scenes.	Student occasionally played their character and environment honestly in their scenes.	Student rarely played their character and environment honestly in their scenes.	Student never played their character and environment honestly in their scenes.
Be in the Present	Student consistently used present tense dialogue and/or object and environment work to keep within the present.	Student occasionally used present tense dialogue and/or object and environment work to keep within the present.	Student rarely used present tense dialogue and/or object and environment work to keep within the present.	Student never used present tense dialogue and/or object and environment work to keep within the present.
Tell a Story	Student consistently utilized the *Important Elements of Storytelling*.	Student occasionally utilized the *Important Elements of Storytelling*.	Student rarely utilized the *Important Elements of Storytelling*.	Student never utilized the *Important Elements of Storytelling*.
Develop Relationships	Student consistently developed relationships and utilized status in their scenes.	Student occasionally developed relationships and utilized status in their scenes.	Student rarely developed relationships and utilized status in their scenes.	Student never developed relationships or utilized status in their scenes.

Appendix F: Additional Game Descriptions

$5 Pyramid
- Get four volunteers who all leave the room.
- While they are out, the class comes up with a list of eight random words. (Suggestions: Items that you would find in a classroom; A place you wouldn't want to go on Spring Break; A word that gives you the heebeegeebees; A food you would order in a restaurant; A color; etc).
- Write the words in two columns of four words each. One column for each team.
- The students who are out of the room decide who will be the "guesser" and who will give the clues.
- Cover the words as the students enter.
- One student from each team sits with their back to the list and their partner faces the list.
- Words are revealed to each team one by one.
- Teams take turns with the "giver" saying word or phrase clues. "Rhymes with" or "sounds like" are not allowed.
- When the guesser figures out a word, the next word on their team list is revealed.
- The teacher acts as host, dinging a bell to switch back and forth between teams.
- The team who finishes their list first wins.

Adverbilies [Video in Bonus Digital Material]
- In this game, students pantomime doing an activity a certain way based on an adverb of the group's choosing.
- Student A leaves the room.
- The rest of the class chooses an adverb (i.e. happily, sadly, hungrily, defiantly).
- A small group is picked to pantomime.
- Student A returns to the room and calls out activities.
- The pantomimers first perform the activity with no emotion.
- Next they perform the activity as the adverb.
  - Example: The group chooses "Happily."
  - Student A: "Show me how you ride a bike."
  - Students pantomime riding a bike with a straight face.
  - Student A: "Now show me riding a bike as your adverb."
  - Students pantomime riding bikes with big smiles on their faces.
  - Student A continues calling out activities until they can guess the adverb.
- Repeat with a new guesser and new pantomimers.

Alphabet
- Ask two players to take the stage and get a suggestion for a scene.
- Students play the scene like any other two person scene, but the first line of dialogue starts with the letter A.
- Each time the other player starts to speak, they must begin their dialogue with the next successive letter of the alphabet.
  - Example: Suggestion: manicure
    - "**A**lan, I wish you would trim your fingernails. They are getting insanely long."

- "**B**ut I need long nails to help untie the kids' shoelaces."
- "**C**andice can figure out how to untie her own shoelaces. People are starting to talk about how creepy your nails are."
- "**D**ads are supposed to be creepy. It is part of the job description."
- etc.

Always Never Also

- Class stands in a circle.
- Teacher turns to the student on their left, endows them with a character name and states that they always or never do something.
- The student accepts the endowment, decides whether that character would be high or low status and replies as that character.
- They add an "also" that goes along with what they always or never do.
- The game continues with each student endowing the person to their left.
  - Example:
    - Teacher: "This is Sylvia. She always pees her pants when she gets excited."
    - Student A: "Well geeze. (Slouches shoulders and speaks in an embarrassed voice). You didn't have to tell everyone. My mom sends me to school with a special bag filled with adult sized diapers. I also pee my pants when I am embarrassed. Um, can I be excused? (Turns to student to their left). This is Ivan. He never forgets to put on his sunscreen."
    - Student B: (Standing up tall and proud, speaking in a know-it-all voice). "My dad told me that I needed to wear sunscreen every day, so I do. Ever since I was 3, I've put on my own sunscreen. I also take a daily vitamin, make my bed, do all my own laundry, and have never missed a day of school, even when I had the measles. Sorry if I got any of you sick. (Turns to the student to their left). This is…"

Audience Add-Ins

- These are two person scenes where audience members (or other students) provide suggestions/dialogue throughout a scene.
- They should all begin as standard two person scenes with any suggestion getting them started.
- Two volunteers stand on stage behind the performers. Each volunteer is assigned to one of the performers.
- As the scene progresses, students stop mid-sentence, and point to their volunteer who supplies an "add-in" (a line of dialogue or a charade). The performer must incorporate that dialogue/charade into the scene.
- Below is a list of all the different versions of "add-ins" that can used in the game:
  - **Pillars**: When prompted by their performer, the volunteer provides one word that the performer repeats and incorporates into the scene.
  - **Sound Effects**: Performers add in elements to the scene that would make noise and volunteers provide the sound effects.
    - Examples:
      - Actor: "I'm going to open this closet door and see what is inside."
      - Volunteer: "Creeeeeeaaaaaak!"
      - Actor: "What an adorable little puppy."
      - Volunteer: "Yip, yip, yip." Or a loud growl
      - Actor: "Let's hop on our Harleys and get out of here."
      - Volunteer: "Vroom, vroom, vroom." Or "Putt putt putt."

- **Three Letter Acronym**: When prompted, the volunteer provides three letters of the alphabet. The performer repeats the three letters then says three words that start with those letters.
  - Example:
    - Student: "Tonight is the night…" (points to volunteer).
    - Volunteer: "AMP"
    - Student: "We get to go to AMP, Another Muppet Performance. They are my absolute favorite."
- **What Text?**: Instruct volunteers to pull out their phones and look up a CLEAN and school appropriate text stream. When prompted, the volunteer provides a random line of dialogue from that text stream.
- **What's Next Charades?**: When prompted, instead of giving a line of dialogue, the volunteer charades a random action. The performer then uses that charade as inspiration for their next line of dialogue.
  - Example:
    - Student: "I can't believe I'm going to…" (points to volunteer).
    - (Volunteer charades rowing a boat).
    - Student: "…to finals with the crew team. This is the year we are going to win."
  - Encourage more advanced students to play off the charade in unexpected ways.
    - Student: "I can't believe I'm going to... (points to volunteer).
    - (Volunteer charades rowing a boat).
    - Student: "..to jail. You sent me up the river Bob! I swear I will get you back for this!"
- **Sentences**: This version does not require any volunteers. Prior to the game, give 8-10 students slips of paper and pens. Instruct them to write a line of dialogue on the paper. Remind students to avoid questions and make strong statements. Performers put the slips of paper in their pockets (Alternately, put all the slips in a bowl on the front of the stage). At any point in the scene, performers pull out a slip of paper and say the sentence as their next line of dialogue.

Automatic Story Telling
- Split the class into two groups.
- Tell everyone that you are going to create a story with one group.
- The other group will ask yes or no questions to guess the details of the story.
- Send one group out of the room.
- Tell the remaining students that the only thing you are going to make up is a story title.
- The students who left the room are going to create the story based on the questions they ask.
- When students from the other group ask questions that begin with a consonant (i.e. "Did the story take place in a palace?") you will all answer "yes."
- When their questions begin with a vowel (i.e. "Are there monkeys involved?") you will all answer "no."
- If you have answered two NO's in a row, the next response is a "yes" regardless of what the question is.
- Bring the first group back into the room.
- Tell them the title of the story.
- They must ask yes or no questions to figure out the location, relationship and story.
- This can be done as a whole class or in partners.
- Once the class or partners come up with a full story, fill them in on the trick.
- Creating a story is not difficult. By "yes, and-ing" you moved the storyline forward.
- It doesn't matter that the stories were ridiculous.
- Ridiculous stories make for good improv scenes.

Barney
- Class stands in a circle with teacher in the middle.
- Round One:
  - When the teacher points to a student, they say their own name, something they sell and a country or city which they sell it.
  - The trick is, all the words have to start with the same letter as their first name.
    - Example: *My name is Mel and I sell melons in Mongolia.*
- Round Two:
  - Player in the middle points to a student and says a random letter, then counts to seven.
  - Student says a random name, item and location that all starts with that letter.
    - Example: "B." *Barney sells bamboo in Botswana.*
  - If the student doesn't say all three things in seven seconds, they become the person in the middle.

Boom Chicago
- Get a suggestion for a conflict.
- Student A creates the environment through pantomime.
- Once it is established where they are, Student B enters the stage and sets up the relationship through one line of dialogue.
- Student A accepts the relationship and creates the conflict through one line of dialogue.
- Student C enters the stage and resolves the conflict through one line of dialogue.
- All students end with "Tadaaaaa."

Bunny, Bunny
- The class stands in a circle.
- There are four movement/sound combos in this game that all happen simultaneously. Start with the first two, then add in three and four as the group gets more comfortable.
  - Movement One: Everyone puts their hands on their knees and bends to a beat while chanting *Room-ba...Room-ba.* (*Room* while bending. *Ba* standing up).
  - Movement Two: Make bunny ears with your pointer and middle fingers on both hands (like the peace sign). Turn your hands towards yourself and bend the fingers twice while saying "Bunny Bunny." Next, turn the fingers to the middle of the circle, make eye contact with a student across the circle and pass the bunny to them by bending your fingers and saying "Bunny Bunny." The student who the bunny was "passed" to says "Bunny Bunny," makes eye contact with another student and passes "Bunny Bunny" to them. While the bunny is passed, all other students are bending at the knees and chanting "Roomba." Once students are passing comfortably, add in the next movement.
  - Movement Three: The students on either side of the "Bunny" student turn towards the Bunny, wave their hands in the air and hop from foot to foot while chanting "Tokki Tokki Tokki Tokki" (Rabbit in Korean). Finally, if your group is super on it, add in the last movement.
  - Movement Four: After passing the bunny to another student, that student puts one hand on their hip, places the other arm straight out to the center of the circle, and says "I passed it. I passed it."

Characters and Objectives
- Round One:
  - Ask three volunteers to take the stage.
  - Endow each person with a very different character (cheerleader, doctor, astronaut, etc).
  - Get a suggestion for a problem that must be solved, such as exterminating cockroaches from a house.

- Students work together to solve the problem, using the strengths of their character.
- Once the problem is solved, the scene is over.
- Round Two:
  - Get four volunteers, a new suggestion and new character endowments.
- Round Three: Five or more students perform. Clump students into groups of characters if needed.

Conducted Story
- Ask 5-8 students to form a horizontal line on stage facing the audience.
- The teacher kneels before the group and acts as conductor.
- The students on the line tell a story based on a suggestion from the audience.
- When the conductor points to a specific student, it is their time to speak.
- When the conductor pulls their hand away, the speaker stops, even if in mid-sentence.
- The conductor points to another student who picks up exactly where the previous student left off.
- Conductor ends the game when the story comes to a "logical" conclusion.
- **Variations:**
  - One Word at a Time: Point to two students with your pointer fingers. When they make eye contact with you, point to one student. That student says the first word. Next point to the other student who says the next word. Go back and forth between the two students. When you are ready to move on, point to a new student to continue the story.
  - Speaking at the Same Time: Point to two students with your pointer fingers. When they make eye contact with you, point your fingers towards each other to indicate they are to speak simultaneously. As long as your fingers are pointing towards each other the students should tell the story in one voice.
  - Elimination Round: If a student does not quickly pick up the story or stumbles with their words, the audience claps their hands twice and shouts "Outta here." The player leaves the line. The remaining students continue the story. The game ends when one student remains.

Cross the Circle
- Class stands in a circle.
- Round One:
  - Teacher makes eye contact with a student across the circle, walks towards that student while saying their name, taps them on the shoulder and takes their place.
  - That student makes eye contact with another student across the circle, says their name, taps their shoulder and takes their place.
  - Once a player has been tapped, they cannot be tapped again.
  - The teacher is the first and last person in the pattern.
  - Run two rounds in this same order, with names.
  - On the third round, students drop names, but continue to make eye contact and tap the shoulder of the student whose spot they take.
- Round Two:
  - Ask the class for a suggestion of a category, such as colors.
  - Assign one student to be the new first person in this pattern.
  - In this round, students do not change places, but continue to make eye contact while saying their word.
    - Example:
      - One student makes eye contact with another student and says "blue."
      - The student who received the "blue" makes eye contact with a new student and says "black."
      - This continues until the last student makes eye contact with first saying their color.

- Round Three:
  - This round is a combination of Rounds One and Two.
  - The teacher starts the first pattern again by making eye contact and tapping the shoulder of the first student from Round One.
  - This pattern continues non-stop.
  - Once students are comfortably changing places, the first student from round two starts their pattern by saying their "color."
  - The next student adds their "color" and so on.
  - Remind students to listen for the "color" before them and also for the "color" after them to make sure that the pattern is not dropped.
- Round Four:
  - If your group seems to have a comfortable grasp on the first three rounds, add in one more category with a new student beginning the pattern.

Deck of Cards
- Utilize a deck of cards to determine characters' status in a scene.
- Ace is lowest status. King is highest status. All other cards are in between.
- These activities can be done as scenes or with students milling about the classroom interacting with their classmates.
- There are three ways the cards can affect a character's status:
  - Option One: Students pick a random card from the deck. The card determines their level of status.
  - Option Two: The card indicates how to treat the other player in the scene.
  - Option Three: Students tape the card to their foreheads so that they cannot see it. They have to figure out their status based on how others react to them.

Enemy Protector
- Each student mentally picks one student to be their enemy and another to be their protector.
- When the game begins, students move themselves so that their protector is standing between them and their enemy at all times.
- Remind the students to avoid physical contact.

Exaggerated Character Walk
- Students mill about the class space and listen to your directions.
- After a few moments, tell them to pick one part of their body that they will start moving slightly differently.
  - Example:
    - Teacher: *"Shoulder."* Students move their shoulder in some fashion. They might roll both shoulders from front to back, may roll shoulders forward or could raise one shoulder to their ear. *"Exaggerate that movement 10%…exaggerate it another 10%…and yet another. Freeze. Think about who you are and why you are walking in this manner? What are you feeling in this moment?"* (If rolling both shoulders back, maybe they are a stressed out college student. Rolling shoulders forward might be the Hunchback of Notre Dame. The one shoulder raiser might indicate they are a ditzy teen who doesn't know the answer to anything). Tell students to have a short conversation with another student, in character.
- Everyone drops their movement and returns to walking normally.
- Pick a new body part to emphasize.
- Repeat for a few rounds.

Foreign Film
- Get a suggestion for the name of a film that has never been made and four volunteers.
- Two students perform a scene from the movie, but can only speak in gibberish.
- The other two students are the translators (one for each actor) who dub the movie into English.
- The actors performing the scene must focus on performing clear object and environment work to create a story. This gives the translators something to go off.
- Gimmicks for translators:
  - Really long translation for short gibberish phrase
  - Really short translation for long gibberish phrase.
  - Play off the opposite of what was expected based on the pantomimed emotion or action.

Freeze
- Class takes the back line.
- Two students start a short scene based on any suggestion.
- Encourage performers to utilize big physical actions in these scenes.
- A student from the line calls "Freeze" when players are in the middle of a big action. Performers freeze in that position.
- The student who called freeze tags out one of the two performers.
- The new student takes the exact position of the tagged out performer and uses associations to come up with a new scene justifying the position they are in.
- If the group is reluctant to call "freeze", or students are calling "freeze" too often, the teacher can call "freeze" and assign students to tag out the players.

Forward Reverse
- Two students perform a scene based on any suggestion.
- After 3-4 lines of dialogue, the teacher calls "reverse."
  The two players work the scene backwards saying the last line of dialogue and then the line before that, etc.
- They also move their bodies backwards through the scene.
- When they return to the start point, the teacher calls forward.
- The students repeat their original lines moving forward.
- At any point, the teacher can call "forward" or "reverse."
- If you have an advanced group, "slow motion" or "switch characters" can be added.
- Encourage students to use big actions.
  - <u>Example</u>:
    - Student A: (Digging up potatoes) "We are so lucky we get to dig up spuds all fall break."
    - Student B: (Crosses the stage, picks up digging fork and joins in the digging). "I know, can you imagine having to go to a beach?"
    - Student A: "No way man."
    - Teacher: "Reverse."
    - Student A: "No way man."
    - Student B: "I know, can you imagine having to go to a beach?" (Puts down digging fork and walks backwards across the stage).
    - Student A: "We are so lucky we get to dig up spuds all fall break."
    - Teacher: "Forward."
    - Student A: "We are so lucky we get to dig up spuds all fall break." Etc...

Goalie
- Students stand in a circle with one student in the middle.
- The student in the middle turns to face one of the outer students.
- The outer student becomes a character and delivers a strong opening line of dialogue. (Ideally indicating relationship and location).
- The student in the middle takes on the corresponding character and responds to the offer.
- After they deliver their response, the student in the middle turns to the next student in the circle who becomes a new character with a new strong opening line of dialogue.
- Center student takes on the new corresponding character and responds.
- Play continues until the student in the middle has received an offer from each student on the outer circle.
- A new student steps into the center of the circle and starts another round.

Great Machine
- One student takes the stage and makes a small gesture with a noise to accompany it.
- Once they have a few moments to do their sound/movement, another student joins them.
- The new student connects themselves to the previous student and adds a new movement and sound.
- The game continues with each student connecting at any point to the machine, one at a time.
- Once everyone is connected, making movements and sounds, the machine is complete.
- Ask one volunteer to explain explain what the machine does and how it works by turning each part on and off individually.
- Begin again with a new student as the originator.

Group Environment
- Split your class into groups of 8-10 students.
- The goal of this game if for the group to create a specific environment one student at a time.
  - Example:
    - Student A opens a door and enters a nondescript room. They turn around and exit the room through the door they entered.
    - Student B opens the same door (making sure it swings the same way), enters the room and interacts with an object of their creation. (i.e. Takes off coat and places on a coat rack or walks to a fridge and pulls out a can of soda). After interacting with their object, they exit through the door.
    - Student C enters through the same door, interacts with Student B's object and introduces their own object.
    - This continues until each student from the group has entered the room, interacted with all previous objects, added in their own object and exited the room.
  - This activity can be used on its own or a two person or group scene can follow.

Half Life
- Get two volunteers and a suggestion for an action from the audience.
- Tell students they have one minute to perform the scene.
- Let them know that strong actions make this game more fun and they need to do an excellent job of listening and remembering.
- After the one minute scene, students perform the same scene, but have only 30 seconds to hit all the major points.
- Next, give them 15 seconds to perform.
- The next scene is 7.5 seconds to get the most essential two to three bits of story performed.

- Finally, give the students 3.75 seconds to communicate THE main plot point.
- With a novice group, allow them to practice all their scenes (1 min, 30 seconds, etc) before performing. Allow advanced groups to improvise their scenes.

Hi-Jacked *[Video in Bonus Digital Material]*
- This is an excellent game for kicking off a show.
- Set up two chairs to represent the front seat of a car.
  - Students partner up and stand behind the chairs.
- Give each set of partners two letters of the alphabet, such as "L and T" or "P and M."
- For the first round, the teacher endows student set one with random characters of their choosing.
- Use an adjective for the first letter and a noun for the second.
  - Example:
    - Teacher: "You are Lazy Teachers."
    - Students enter the car as lazy teachers.
    - Passenger: "I just gave the students the answer sheets before the test and told them to go ahead and use it to grade their own final exams."
    - Driver: "I recently discovered pbskids.org. Who needs to teach when you can play Mr. Rogers all day?"
    - Passenger: "I'm planning on sending one of my students in my stead to the statewide standards conference."
    - Teacher claps or rings the bell. (Allow a few lines of dialogue for students to create their characters).
    - Driver: "Oh no! We're being hijacked by..." and utilizes their two letters of the alphabet to endow the next partnership with their characters.
    - This continues until each partnership gets at least one round in the car.
- This game breaks the side rule of trying not to be funny. Because of this game's fast pace, students can and should throw out silly one liners that pertain to their endowment. Listening to your scene partner is still extremely important in order to build the humor and play the game within the game.

Hint Away
- The class stands on the back line.
- Get a suggestion for a well known person, object, location, animal, etc.
- As ideas come to them, students step forward and make a hint through dialogue and/or pantomime. When the student finishes their hint, they step back and another student steps forward.
  - Example: The ring from Lord of the Rings:
    - "Oh isn't this precious" (Pantomime putting on a ring).
    - "If our marriage is "doomed", then I'm throwing this into the heart of a mountain!"
    - "Sam, it's your turn to wear it!"
  - Example: Dory from Finding Nemo:
    - "Don't tell me…I know I know this."
    - (Pantomime opening a newspaper). "Honey, the perfect job for you…the school needs a whale translator!"
    - "I know I look blue, but really, I'm not so sad."

Interrogators

- Set up two chairs on the stage about 5 feet apart facing the audience.
- Get four volunteers and send two of them out of the room. They will be those accused of a crime. The two volunteers remaining in the room are the cops.
- While they are gone, the class comes up with the crime. A prominent person (from history, pop culture, etc) has been killed in a specific, well known location with a famous object.
  - Example: *Abraham Lincoln was killed on the Hollywood Walk of Fame with the Ruby Slippers from the Wizard of Oz.*
- Call the two accused back into the room.
- They sit in the chairs.
- Each accused has one cop who interrogates them.
- One at a time, the cops grill the accused about who they murdered. The accused deny any wrong doing.
- After one or two hints from Cop 1, the teacher dings the bell and the other cop gets a chance. This goes back and forth throughout the game.
- Having two cops is especially helpful for guessing because the accused gets two sets of clues.
- When the accused thinks they know "who" the murdered is, they say, "Move on copper, I ain't got all day."
- The cop begins giving clues about the location.
- Once one of the accused thinks they know all three elements, they call it out. "I didn't kill Abe Lincoln on the Walk of Fame with Dorthy's slippers."
- If they get it right, game over.
- If they get something wrong, cop should let them know what was wrong and continue giving clues.
  - Example:
    - Cop 1: You know why I brought you in here? Thought your *four scores* would go unnoticed?" (Ding)
    - Accused 1: "I ain't done nothing wrong!"
    - Cop 2: "You thought you could escape to the theater for a night, eh?" (Ding)
    - Accused 2: "You got no cause to bring me in!"
    - Cop 1: One of those beard hairs was found on your jacket. Explain that?" (Ding)
    - Cop 2: "Get that top hat off your head when I'm talking to you!"
    - Accused 2: "Move on copper."
    - Cop 2: "Thought you'd see stars if you committed this crime, eh"
    - Other possible clues for Hollywood Walk of Fame: "Imagined your name up in giant letters on the side of a hill?" "You like hanging out in front of Chinese theaters?"
    - Clues for shoes: "*There's no place* like a jail cell for you!" "Thought you'd hide the evidence under a house?" "Clicking those heel cuffs together ain't gonna send you home!"

Let's Not

- This game is good for more advanced groups who are ready to play with the rule of "yes, and" not being a literal "yes, and" to every bit of dialogue.
- This game also helps teach the idea of going with the flow and dropping your expectation of where the story should go.
- Partner up students.
- Give each partnership the same location.
- Partners play this game telling a story based on the location one sentence at a time.
- After one student has given the other an offer, their partner can either accept it or deny it.

- Offers should only be denied if they do not advance the story or if the other player has an amazing alternative that would advance the story.
- Share stories with the class.
- Discuss how many different stories came from the same suggestion.
  - Example:
    - Student A: "Let's hit up the the ski hill this afternoon."
    - Student B: "Yes, let's do that. I just got a new snowboard. I want to try it out."
    - Student A: "Yes, I've been dying to go down the triple black diamond shoots."
    - Student B: "Let's not head over to the shoots. I spent months saving up for this board and don't want to break it. I was thinking maybe we could hit up the bunny slopes to try it out."
    - Student A: "Um, the bunny slopes are for babies. Let's at least head over to the terrain park. You can ride past all the elements and I could hit up the rails."

Lie to Me
- Two students take the stage.
- Ask the class for a close relationship, such as siblings or classmates.
- Ask them about a mischievous activity that the two actors have been a part of.
  - Examples:
    - How did Sammy end up covered in tar and feathers?
    - Why am I getting phone calls from the FBI about you two?
    - How on earth did our piano end up in the vegetable garden?
    - (See more examples at http://www.bbbpress.com/2016/03/drama-game-tell-a-lie/).
- One student takes the lead and begins the story by telling what led up to the mischievous event taking place.
- After a few lines of dialogue, they turn to their partner in crime who then continues the story.
- This back and forth continues for the remainder of the story.
- The two students make themselves look like innocent bystanders or like they were mistakingly caught up in the event.
- At any point, students in the class can raise their hand to ask questions for clarification or to move the story along.

Luckily Unluckily
- Similar to "Yes, and."
- Students will go around the circle telling a story alternating between "Luckily" and "Unluckily."
- Good for a more advanced group to show how blocking can be frustrating, but when done as part of "the game" can lead to very humorous outcomes.
- The teacher begins with a strong opening statement.
  - Example:
    - Teacher: "School lunch today is moldy meatloaf."
    - Student A (to the teacher's right, adds a sentence starting with luckily): "Luckily I brought my own lunch."
    - Student B (adds in the unluckily): "Unluckily, the school bully broke into my locker and stole it."
    - Student C: "Luckily, it was open campus Friday so I was able to leave to buy lunch at Taco Bell."
    - Student D: "Unluckily, the health inspector closed down Taco Bell because their meat was getting people sick."
- Continues around the circle once or twice, with the last students wrapping up the story.

MacGyver [Video in Bonus Digital Material]
- Explain that MacGyver was originally a television show in the 1980's where the main character, a secret agent named MacGyver, got out of life threatening situations with ordinary objects.
- For this game you will need two volunteers and suggestions for three everyday objects (such as a glove, scissors and a comic book).
- You also need a suggestion for a life threatening situation (such as being chased by bears or kidnapped by international terrorists).
- The students use those objects to save themselves in an improvised scene.
- In addition to the three objects, students can utilize a Swiss Army knife and duct tape, because MacGyver always had those items on hand.

Madison Avenue
- Four students take the stage.
- Get a suggestion for an adjective and a noun.
- This is the object for an advertising campaign.
- The campaign needs a slogan, packaging, a famous spokesperson, and a commercial jingle.
- As students come up with ideas (starting with the slogan), the other players accept the idea, say how wonderful it is and add to why it is such a great idea.
- Game continues with "yes, and"-ing the ideas until all students are singing along with the created jingle.
  - Example: Silly Carpet.
    - Student A: "'Silly Carpet: The rug that keeps you laughing all day long.'"
    - All: "Yes that is amazing."
    - Student B: "I think the silly carpet should be sold in a carpet bag, like Mary Poppins carried around."
    - All: "Yes, that is awesome."
    - Student C: "My great uncle was Walt Disney. I can get the actual bag from the movie!"
    - All: "Perfect!"
    - Student B: "You know who would be perfect to be the spokesperson? John Travolta because he wears a toupee which is also called a rug."
    - Student D: "And John Travolta was hysterical in Greece and Pulp Fiction, so people will really believe that he thinks the carpet is funny."
    - All: "Brilliant"
    - Student A: "I have an idea for the jingle. (Singing) 'When life has got you down and your floors are a sticky mess. Don't just tarp it…go on down and get a Silly Carpet!"
    - All: "Go on down and get a Silly Carpet!"

Malapropism
- <u>Round One</u>: Students walk around the room, point to objects and call them by gibberish names.
  - Example: Point to a chalk board and call it a "huphenbopen."
- <u>Round Two</u>: Students walk around the room, point to objects and call them by other names.
  - Example: Point to a chalk board and call it a "pencil."
- <u>Round Three</u>: Students call objects by words that sound similar.
  - Example: Point to a chalk board and call it a "block fjord."

Mime Whispers [Video in Bonus Digital Material]
- Students think of an everyday activity, such as brushing their teeth.

- They break that activity into six motions, numbering each pantomime.
  - Example:
    - One: Take cap off toothpaste.
    - Two: Squeeze toothpaste on brush.
    - Three: Put down toothpaste tube.
    - Four: Brush teeth.
    - Five: Spit.
    - Six: Turn on water to rinse off brush.
- Remind students of good habits for object work. Example: put down the toothpaste tube before brushing. Don't let it disappear out of your hand.
- Partner up students.
- In pairs students share their pantomime, but don't say what they are doing.
- Students can ask their partner to redo the six motions one extra time.
- After that, if the partner is unsure of the pantomime, they make a judgement call as to what it most looked like.
- After both students have performed their pantomimes, they find a new partner.
- Students share the pantomime they observed with a new partner.
- If you have time, partner students up for a third round of sharing.
- Gather students in a circle.
- Each student shares the last pantomime they observed.
- The class guesses the activity.

Monty Python Tag
- This is an "everybody's it" game.
- When the teacher gives the word, students become the black knight from the movie Monty Python and the Holy Grail.
- They WALK (not run) around the classroom space using their sword (pointer finger) to try and tag other knights.
- If a knight gets tagged once, they lose that arm (bend it behind their back). They can still tag other knights with their other hand.
- Get tagged twice and they lose both arms, but are still in the game.
- Get tagged three times and they lose one leg and hop around the room on one leg trying to avoid getting tagged again.
- Get tagged a fourth time, they kneel on the ground.
- At this point, their job is to taunt the other players in their worst British accent with lines such as "Come back and fight." "It's only a flesh wound." "The Black Knight always triumphs!" "Chicken."
- The game ends when one player is left with at least one arm.

Musical Chairs
- Choose 6-8 students to take the stage.
- Get a suggestion for a scene.
- This game starts like a regular game of musical chairs set up in a circle. One less chair than there are students.
- Play music while students dance around the chairs. After a minute or so, stop the music. Students scramble to get a chair. The student without a chair, removes their chair from the stage and joins the audience.
- The remaining students play a scene, in front of the chairs, based on the initial suggestion.

- Once the scene has come to a good editing point (is well established and/or hits an especially humorous note), start the music again.
- Students go back to walking around the chairs.
- Stop the music. Students scramble to get a chair. The student without a chair, removes their chair from the stage and joins the audience.
- The remaining students play a scene based on the initial suggestion or inspired by the previous scene.
- The game continues in this fashion until there are two players remaining.
- Have one final round of musical chairs with the last seated player claiming prize as the winner. (The prize is bragging rights for exactly 15 seconds).

Ninja Star, Sleeping Kitten, Angry Chihuahua

- Have the class silently walk around the classroom.
- Tell the students they are going to mime passing different objects from person to person as they walk through the space.
- To pass an object, they must make eye contact with the person they are passing to.
- Begin by making eye contact with a student and throwing them a ninja star. Make a "ninja" like sound as you throw the star.
- The receiver stealthily catches the star and it continues being thrown from student to student until everyone has had it at least once.
- Pause the game and add in the sleeping kitten. Remind students they do not want to wake the kitten. As the kitten is tossed, make a purring noise.
- The ninja star continues to be thrown while the kitten is getting tossed.
- Finally, pause the game to add in the angry chihuahua with a "yip yip!" Remind students that chihuahuas have sharp teeth and bite when angry.
- Reflect on how each of the objects were passed differently.
- Feel free to take student suggestions of other objects that can be passed.

Nuclear Bomb Chicken

- Round One:
  - Gather students in a standing circle.
  - Tell them they are chickens at a farm and must play them as honestly as possible.
  - After 30 seconds, call "Freeze."
  - Explain that in another 30 seconds, a nuclear bomb is going to drop at the farm.
  - Tell the students to continue acting like chickens.
  - End the exercise and gather students in a sitting circle.
  - Discuss the initial rule of the game: *Play the chickens as honestly as possible.* If students were acting as chickens honestly, they would not have acknowledged that the bomb was arriving because chickens do not know about bombs! The reality of the character is sometimes different from the reality of the player.
- Round Two:
  - Discuss playing animals and other non-human characters in scenes.
  - The player can portray a talking chicken, but should do so with all the characteristics of a chicken (small brain/dumb, fighting over pecking order, hens are broody, roosters are 'cocky').
  - Give a few minutes for students to walk around acting like chickens.
  - Signal for them to have a conversation with another student speaking honestly as chickens.
  - Regather and have students share a few of the conversations.

The Oracle [Video in Bonus Digital Material]
- Ask four students to form a line going from downstage to upstage, one in back of the other, in the following formation:
  - The first player sits on floor, legs criss-crossed.
  - The second sits behind them in a chair.
  - The third stands behind the chair.
  - The fourth stands on a chair in the back.
- Audience asks the Oracle questions, such as "What should I dress as next year for Halloween?" or "What college am I going to go to?"
- Each member of the oracle can only answer the question one word at a time.
- Game starts with the student on the floor saying the first word, the student in the chair saying the second word and so on.
- After the student standing on the chair adds their word, the student on the floor continues with the next word, and so on.
- Encourage listening to every word to make complete thoughts and limiting "ands" and "because" so that the answer does not go on forever.
- The answer ends when a student decides the person before them added a good final word.
- When the Oracle hears silence for more than a few seconds, they know they have answered the question and each student lowers their head together.
- The Oracle's answers may not make perfect sense, but the Oracle is ALWAYS right.

Pass the Clap with Words
- Class stands in a circle.
- Round One:
  - Teacher turns to the student to their right (Student A) and makes eye contact.
  - Teacher and Student A clap simultaneously.
  - Student A turns to the student to their right (Student B) and makes eye contact.
  - Student A and Student B clap simultaneously.
  - This continues around the circle.
  - Slow the students down if they are getting sloppy.
  - Once the clap has gone around the circle two or three times, pass the clap around the circle in the other direction.
- Round Two:
  - Choose a category, such as "sports."
  - Teacher turns to the student on their right and slowly says a sport.
  - As soon as Student A figures out what sport the teacher is saying, they join in.
    - Example: "Foooooootball."
  - Student A turns to Student B and says a different sport in the same manner.
  - This continues around the circle.
  - Once the category has gone around the circle once, repeat with the same words two more times.
- Round Three:
  - Start a new category, such as fruit.
    - Example: "Strawberry"
    - Run two times.
- Round Four:
  - Start this round with the first category (sports).
  - Once that category is half way around the circle, add in the second category (fruit.)
  - Remind students to listen for their words and make eye contact.

- Remind students it will not work if they do not connect with their partner.
- Additional Rounds: If your group is especially adept (or large), try adding in a third or fourth category.

Ping Pong
- Ask for four volunteers to take the stage and get a suggestion for the scene.
- Get ten lines of random dialogue from the class or choose ten lines from Appendix C: Opening Lines of Dialogue/Lines for Sentences.
- Write each line on the board and label them 1-10.
- Two of the students perform a scene based on the suggestion, while the other two volunteers watch from the side.
- Each performer must use one line of dialogue from the list, in order 1-10, before the next performer can begin their dialogue.
- The scene ends when line 10 of dialogue is spoken.
- The two students waiting, now perform a new scene based on the suggestion.
- They also use the same ten lines of dialogue, but in the opposite order 10-1.
- Encourage the performers to come up with different uses for the same dialogue.
- The game ends when line 1 of dialogue is spoken.
  - Example: Random Dialogue Lines
    - 1. Santa doesn't love you.
    - 2. I want a golden goose.
    - 3. Look at the camera and say 'fuzzy pickle.'
    - etc.
  - Example Scene:
    - Student A: "Veronica, it doesn't matter if you do good things, Santa doesn't love you."
    - Student B: " I don't understand why! I should be on the good list. I gave you my cookie today at lunch. It is't fair. I want a golden goose for Christmas!"
    - Student A: "Well maybe if you sit on his lap at the mall and look at the camera and say 'fuzzy pickle' he will take pity on you and give you your golden goose."

Puppets
- Ask four players to take the stage and get a suggestion for a scene.
- Two players are the puppets and two are the puppet masters.
- The puppets deliver the dialogue based on the suggestion, but are unable to move their bodies.
- The puppet masters move the puppets' bodies into positions.
- Remind puppet masters to be gentle with their puppets.
- If they want their puppet to wave hello, the puppet master lifts the puppet's arm.
- If they want them to nod yes, they take the puppets head and tilt it (gently) up and down.
- To get the puppets to walk, the master taps the back of the puppet's knees.
- Play a round of Puppet's Revenge where the puppets are masters and the masters are puppets.

Same Opener, Different Scene
- Get an opening line of dialogue from the audience.
- Two volunteers perform a scene using that line of dialogue.
- Let the students develop the scene enough to show their environment, relationship and conflict.
- Choose three new volunteers to perform an unrelated scene using the same opening line of dialogue.
- Again, let it run to show environment, relationship and conflict.
- Finally, get four volunteers to perform an unrelated scene using the same opening line of dialogue.

Silent Scenes
- Ask two volunteers to perform a short two person scene.
- For beginner students, give them a full premise of a scene.
  - Example: You are a brother and a sister. You are playing ball in the house and one of you breaks a lamp. You need to deal with it before your parents get home.
- For more advanced students, just get a suggestion for the scene.
- These scenes are played without dialogue.
- Performers use pantomime to communicate actions and emotions.

Superheroes
- Ask four students to take the stage.
- Tell one student (Student A) to stay on the stage and the other three to stand off to the side.
- The class endows Student A with a ridiculous and detailed superhero name, such as "Cries at the Drop of a Hat Man."
- The class also gives Student A a problem to solve, such as exterminating cockroaches from their house.
- Student A starts the scene with a strong initiation, in the character of their superhero, but fails to solve the problem. (Example: "I must rid this home of cockroaches. A roach motel, that is what I need. (Sobbing). My ex-girlfriend broke up with me at a motel. I can't do this alone.")
- They call in the Student B, and endow them with a superhero name (Example: "I need my best friend, Crazy Cat Lady!")
- Student B enters and attempts to help through their character's strength. ("I can eat the cockroaches like I do mice! Hmmmm, bad idea. Too crunchy.")
- When Student B fails to solve the problem, Student C enters the scene. Student B endows Student C with a superhero name.
- Student C fails to solve the problem.
- Finally Student D enters, gets endowed by Student C and comes up with the perfect solution for solving the problem.

Three Line Scene
- Students split into two columns facing the audience.
- The first two students of the columns step forward.
- Student from the Stage Left line starts a scene with dialogue that sets up a relationship. "Marge, I'm sick of eating spaghetti every night for dinner."
- Student from Stage Right line accepts this dialogue and further adds to the relationship. "Frank, I thought the spaghetti would remind you of our honeymoon in Italy."
- Stage left actor finishes the scene with a 3rd line of dialogue. "Italy was your idea. I wanted to spend our honeymoon in Cleveland."
- After the 3rd line of dialogue, students go to the back of the opposite column so that everyone gets a chance to initiate a scene.
- Continue until each student has been in both columns.
- If you have an advanced class talk about the second actor not taking on the obvious relationship. For instance, instead of Marge being a wife, maybe she was a jail guard bringing dinner to an inmate. "Marge, I'm sick of eating spaghetti every night for dinner." "Well Frank, you should have thought about that before you got yourself sent up here to prison." "How was I to know I'd be so bad at robbing banks."

Threesome

- One student steps up to the stage, states they are a random object, then strikes a pose as that object. Example: "I am a slice of cheese."
- A second student joins and strikes a pose as a complimenting object. "I am a hamburger patty."
- A third player joins them and completes the trio. "I am a bun."
- All three players exit the stage and a new student starts the next round.

Three Words: Why Sorry Oh

- Divide the class into groups of two or three.
- Round One:
  - Groups get a few minutes to plan a pantomimed scene with a beginning, middle and end.
  - The catch is, they can only use the words "Why" "Oh" and "Sorry."
  - Have each group perform their scene. Assign each group another group to pay extra attention to for Round Two.
- Round Two:
  - Students recreate another group's scene, but are allowed to speak.
  - Give the groups a few minutes to discuss and rehearse.
  - Have each group perform.
  - After the spoken scenes, the original group shares what their silent scene was actually about.

Translate Gibberish

- Class stands/sits in a circle.
- Teacher turns to the student to their right, Student A, and says a line of dialogue in gibberish (a nonsensical, made up language).
- Student A then "translates" the sentence into English for the rest of the class.
- Next, Student A turns to the student on their right, Student B, and speaks a line in their own gibberish.
- Student B translates the line of dialogue into English for the class.
- Game continues around the circle.
- Encourage students to speak with emotion and hand gestures to give their translator something to go off of with their translation.
- If you have a more advanced group, encourage them to play off opposites. Example: If the student speaking gibberish was laughing as they spoke, translate a very sad story. If the sentence was extremely long, make the translation super short or vice versa. This is a good practice game if you intend to play Foreign Film.

Two Headed Scene

- Ask for four volunteers to take the stage and create two pairs.
- Each pair will become one two-headed character as they perform a scene.
- Partners should link arms to make them one person.
- One pair speaks in one voice (speak simultaneously).
- The other pair speaks one word at a time.

Yes, and

- This game can be played as a whole class sitting in a circle or in partners.
- The teacher starts the game with a strong initiation statement.

- Example: "This is the ugliest pair of cowboy boots that I have ever seen."
- If playing as a class, everyone shares in telling a whole group story.
- The student to the teacher's right, Student A, continues the story starting with the phrase, "Yes, and…"
  - Example: "Yes, and we're going to wear them for ugly shoe day this Friday."
- The next student continues the story.
  - Example: "Yes and we're going to win the contest for worst shoes."
- The game continues with each student in the circle adding to the story, with the last few wrapping it up.
- If playing in partners, "Yes, and" is a conversation between two students going back and forth.
- Encourage students to include a conflict.
  - Example:
    - Student A: "Yes and I am going to wear them for ugly shoe day this Friday."
    - Student B: "Yes and I am going to wear my silver and gold studded Mary Janes."
    - Student A: "Yes and I am going to win because my boots are more hideous than yours."
    - Student B: "Yes and I am going to laugh at you when you limp up to get your award because you have terrible blisters from wearing those awful boots."
- Partner conversations go on for several minutes.

Yes, Let's

- Get a suggestion for a group activity, such as playing a sport or having a birthday party.
- Students take turns coming forward as they get ideas saying, "Let's..." They state the activity while pantomiming it.
- Once a student has stepped forward, they remain on stage and join in the new pantomimes that other students come up with.
  - Example:
    - Student A: "Let's hit the piñata." Pantomimes blindly striking a stick at the piñata.
    - Student B steps up to the stage: "Yes, let's!" Pantomimes putting a blindfold on them-self, picking up a stick and whacking the stick in the air. Takes off blindfold and says, "Let's play pin the tail on the donkey."
    - Student A: "Yes Let's!" Student A pantomimes placing a blindfold on Student B who then tries to pin a tail on the donkey.
    - Student C steps up the the stage: "Let's sing happy birthday."
    - Students A and B: "Yes Let's!" (A, B and C sing happy birthday).
  - Game continues until all students are on stage.

Yes No Banana Please

- Divide your class into partners.
- Each partnership creates a short scene with a location, characters, a beginning-middle-end as well as a conflict.
- The catch is they can only use the words "yes" "no" "banana" and "please" in their dialogue.
- They may use any combination of these words in one sentence, but they may not use any other words.
- Give the class 3-5 minutes to practice, then share.

You're Fired
- Two players perform the following script.
  - Student A: (Knocks on door).
  - Student B: "Come in. You know why I called you?"
  - Student A: (Miming that they don't know why).
  - Student B: (Mimes handing Student A a piece of paper).
  - Student A: "I thought you wouldn't take that into account?"
  - Student B: "You're fired."
  - Student A: "Fine. I hated that worthless job anyway."
- Once they have performed the scene straight, the teacher or the class give endowments to the performers.
  - Options:
    - Change your emotions (happy, depressed, annoyed, etc).
    - You are wearing clothes that do not fit.
    - You are a specific animal.
    - You are 80 years old.
    - The other character makes you feel a certain way (you think they are cute, you think they are ugly, you like how they smell, etc).
  - The students perform the script again (verbatim) with the endowment.
  - Encourage students to make the scene their own through status changes and lots of environment/object work and pantomiming.
  - Remind them to think about what is written on the note.
  - Specifics are what make scenes real.

Zen Counting
- Class stands in a circle with backs facing into the circle. '
- The objective is to see how high you can count as a group.
- Students take turns saying numbers 1, 2, 3 and so on.
- The rules:
  - You cannot simply go around the circle in order.
  - You cannot plan the order.
  - If two students speak at the same time, the group starts back at 1.
- See how high you can get.
- This is a game of listening and give and take.

Zone-Ra
- Get three different suggestions to assign to stage left, center and right.
- Suggestions: film/theater style (horror, musical, drama, etc), emotions, accents (if your students can pull them off, or if you want a good laugh), careers, locations, ways of communicating (sign language, pantomime, puppeteering), etc.
  - Example:
    - Stage left = musical
    - Center stage =- frustrated
    - Stage right = French accent
- Get two volunteers and a suggestion for the scene.
- As students move around the stage, they change their performance based on where they are.
- If they are standing in stage left, they sing their dialogue.

- When in center stage, all their dialogue is said in a frustrated tone.
- When in stage right, they speak in a French accent.
- Students should move about the stage as naturally as possible.
- A gimmick of this game is to walk across the stage speaking one continuous bit of dialogue, hitting all three zones.
- Another gimmick is to straddle two zones.
  - Example: Singing a frustrated bit of dialogue or speaking in a frustrated French accent.

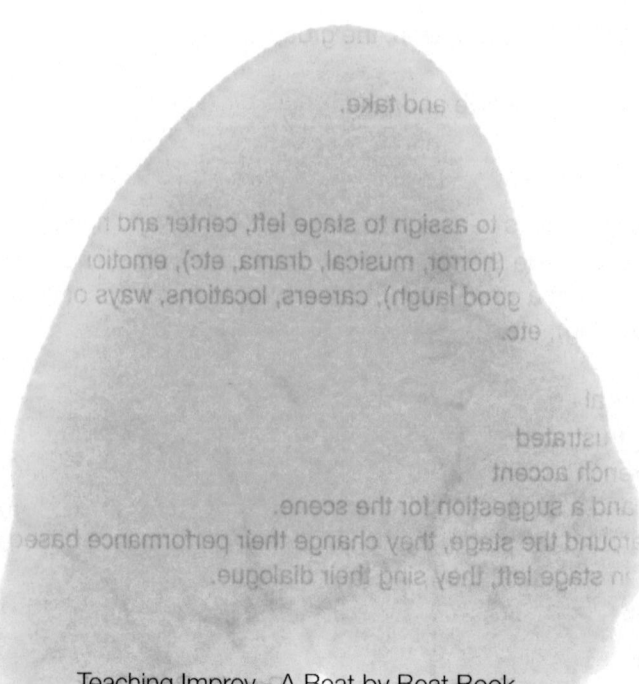

Appendix G: Glossary of Terms

Blocking: To deny another player's offer.

Edit: To interrupt or end a scene.

Endow: To give another player or players physical, emotional or other characteristics. Ex: You are a clown who likes to pick his nose.

Environment Work: The act of creating the "where" in a scene through pantomime. i.e. opening a door, turning on a faucet, etc.

Get: A suggestion for starting a scene.

Gift: Any strong offer that a performer presents to their scene partner. These can be strong statements with information, an emotional reaction and/or specific environment/object work that states where you are and what you are doing.

Group Mind: When a group is listening and relating to each other so well that they seem to work as one. Their movements may be in conjunction or their ideas are so in sync that the creation of a scene appears seamless.

Heightening: Adding information that raises the stakes in a scene and makes it more interesting.

Justifying: To make sense of an offer in a scene.

Pantomime: The act of communicating an action or an emotion without words.

Object Work: The act of miming the use of non-existent objects. i.e. folding a towel, shooting a basketball, etc.

Offer: Statements, object or environment work that moves a scene forward.

Playing the Game within the Game: The "game" is a pattern that evolves within a scene and playing it is to continue the pattern and heighten it.

Status: The power difference between two people.

Tag Out: When a scene is taking place and a new player tags someone and takes their place in a scene.

Taking the Back Line: When players stand along the back wall of the stage facing the audience. Scenes take place in front of these players. Players take turns stepping forward to start scenes, join scenes, tag out players or edit scenes.

Tableau: Actors freezing in a pose to represent a specific place or moment. Usually they are created by getting a suggestion for a location and actors stepping out one at a time to become objects or people found in that location.

Walk-on: When a player enters a scene, makes a strong offer to heighten the scene and then exits.

Appendix H: Bibliography, Resources, Acknowledgements

Bibliography

Alda, Alan. *If I Understood You, Would I Have This Look on My Face?: My Adventures in the Art and Science of Relating and Communicating.* New York: Random House, 2018.

Bany-Winters, Lisa. *On Stage: Theater Games and Activities for Kids.* Chicago: Chicago Review Press, Inc., 1997.

Bedore, Bob. *101 Improv Games for Children and Adults.* Alameda: Hunter House Inc., Publishers, 2004.

Boyke, Guido, Improvwiki. https://improwiki.com/en. Accessed March 17, 2019.

Browdy, Gil, & Vinny Francois. Can I Get A… http://www.can-i-get-a.com. Accessed March 17, 2019.

Buchanan, Matt. "Improvs and Warmups." Child Drama. https://www.childdrama.com/warmups.html. Accessed March 17, 2019.

Business Dictionary. http://www.businessdictionary.com. Accessed March 17, 2019.

Carrane, Jimmy. Jimmy Carrane Honest Comedy. http://jimmycarrane.com/blog. Accessed March 17, 2019.

Casado, Denver. "Drama Games for Kids." Beat by Beat Press. http://www.bbbpress.com/dramagames. Accessed March 17, 2019.

Casado, Denver. *Teaching Drama: The Essential Handbook.* San Francisco: Beat by Beat Press, 2014.

Close, Del, Charna Halpern & Kim Howard Johnson. *Truth in Comedy: The Manual for Improvisation.* Colorado Springs: Meriwether Publishing, 1994.

Cambridge Dictionary. https://dictionary.cambridge.org. Accessed March 17, 2019.

Crawford, Trace. *Absolutely Everything**You Need to Know About Teaching and Performing Improv.* Columbus: Electric Whirligig Press, 2015.

English Oxford Living Dictionary. https://en.oxforddictionaries.com. Accessed March 17, 2019.

Espeland, Todd. "High Status/Low Status Character Physicality." *Theatre Folk.* https://www.theatrefolk.com/blog/high-statuslow-status-character-physicality. Accessed March 17, 2019.

Ezis, Aaron. "Short Stories for Children." American Literature. 1997 https://americanliterature.com. Accessed March 17, 2019.

Farmer, David. *Learning Through Drama in the Primary Years*. Norwich: Drama Resource, 2011.

Funk, Joshua. "What the Hell is 'Clumping?'" The Second City Hollywood. https://www.facebook.com/notes/second-city-hollywood/what-the-hell-is-clumping/151349011563297. Accessed March 17, 2019.

Gantz, Patrick. Improv as Improv Does Best. https://improvdoesbest.com. Accessed March 17, 2019.

Goldstein, Dan. "How to Be a Better Improvisor." 2009. DanGoldstein.com. http://www.dangoldstein.com/howtoimprovise.html. Accessed March 17, 2019.

Hall, William. Improv Games. 2018. http://www.improvgames.com/category/games/. Accessed March 17, 2019.

The Improv Page. http://www.improvcomedy.org. Accessed March 17, 2019.

Jagodowski, TJ and Dave Pasquesi. *Improvisation at the Speed of Life*. New York: Solo Roma, Inc. 2015.

Johnstone, Keith. *Impro: Improvisation and Theater*. Abingdon: Routledge: 1987.

Jones, David K. "5 Improv Exercises to be a Better Listener." April 1, 2015. Think Fast Improv. http://www.thinkfastimprov.com/blog/5-improv-exercises-to-be-a-better-listener. Accessed 27 April 2018. Internet Archive. https://web.archive.org/web/20160923141301/http://www.thinkfastimprov.com/blog/5-improv-exercises-to-be-a-better-listener. Accessed March 17, 2019.

Jones, David K. "My New Favorite Improv Warm-Up Game." April 22, 2014. Think Fast Improv. http://thinkfastimprov.com/blog/my-new-favorite-improv-warm-up-game. Accessed March 17, 2019.

Off Camera with Sam Jones. "Keegan-Michael Key: Improv Actors Are at War Together." YouTube, Accessed March 17, 2019, https://youtu.be/KmCsoGrz5QI.

Off Camera with Sam Jones. "Matt Walsh Reveals His Keys to Improv." YouTube. Accessed March 17, 2019. https://youtu.be/0ispdtG_TIA.

MacLeod, Hugh. Learn Improv. 2018. https://learnimprov.com. Accessed March 17, 2019.

McKnight, Katherine S. & Mary Scruggs. *The Second City Guide to Improv in the Classroom*. San Francisco: Jossey-Bass, 2008.

Merriam Webster Dictionary. https://www.merriam-webster.com. Accessed March 17, 2019.

Mullany, Kevin. "Status Exercise in Improv." Kevin Mullany: Theater, books, improv, poker, food and dementia. 2015. https://kevinmullaney.com/2015/11/16/status-exercises-in-improv. Accessed March 17, 2019.

Mullany, Kevin. "Take an Exercise, Leave an Exercise." Improv Resource Center. https://improvresourcecenter.com/forums/index.php?threads/take-an-exercise-leave-an-exercise.1982/. Accessed March 17, 2019.

Smallwood, Cameron and Sally "Wanna Be Funny, Don't Try to Act Funny." People and Chairs. https://peopleandchairs.com/2013/03/28/wanna-be-funny-dont-try-to-act-funny/. Accessed March 17, 2019.

Spolin, Viola. *Theater Games for the Classroom: A Teacher's Handbook*. Evanston: Northwestern University Press, 1963.

Tollenaere, Tom. Improv Encyclopedia. 2018. https://www.improvencyclopedia.org. Accessed March 17, 2019.

Facebook Groups:

Below are three great improv groups on Facebook with members who are open and wiling to share advice, ideas and suggestions. "Improvisational theater - group for players worldwide," is a global forum for improvisors moderated by Tom Tollenaere, the man behind the online site Improv Encyclopedia. Improv Teachers' Support & Collaboration Group is dedicated to teachers of improv. Applied Improvisation Network is a community of practitioners who apply improv to build life skills in communities and organizations.

Tollenaere, Tom. "Improvisational Theater - group for players worldwide." https://www.facebook.com/groups/worldwideimprov.

Hansen, Leif. "Applied Improvisation Network." https://www.facebook.com/groups/appliedimprov

Victor, Pam. "Improv Teachers' Support & Collaboration Group." https://www.facebook.com/groups/565158500303589.

Additional Video Clips

> **DISCLAIMER:** Some, but not all, of these videos have a quick swear word or a small amount of humor (less than 15 seconds) that may not be appropriate for younger classes. I add them here because they are great examples of fun games not included in the book, have quality performances that are worth sharing or include valuable instruction to share with your class. Please view them beforehand and use at your own discretion.

Whose Line Is It Anyway: Let's Make a Date
Unofficial Video Clip: https://youtu.be/MWA7DONUG8Q
Official Video Full Episode: (game starts at 1:06) https://bit.ly/2DHT9oG

Improv-A-Ganza: Sentences - As the Jack Flaps
https://youtu.be/blbpwFuZQqA

Improv-A-Ganza: Read Ending Car Accident
https://youtu.be/35cbfkvYh-Q

Roman Improv Games: Translator Impaired
https://youtu.be/uOG4FD2X5MQ

Roman Improv Games: Rhyming New Choice (Start 00:56 into the clip)
https://youtu.be/cFbHB7bZuyY?t=56

Whose Line Is It Anyway: Old Job, New Job
https://youtu.be/TMVW-5adxYA

Improv-A-Ganza: Moving People (Price is Right Models - Fencing)
https://youtu.be/D21_BoevY0I

Eight is Never Enough: Authors (aka Conducted Story)
https://youtu.be/t6rxT3_buqA

Acknowledgments

The lessons put forth in this book were formulated over years of teaching, improvising and writing. There are countless people who lent an ear to an idea, an eye to a rewrite or a body and imagination to a game. First and foremost, I need to thank the past and present members of the Laff Staff, my improv troupe. Thanks for all that you have taught me and for having my back throughout the years. Special thanks to Nick, Kjera, Josh, John, Jackie, Chris and Brian for being a part of this book. Thank you to Dani, Kristin and all the teachers and parents who have allowed me to work with your children and try out new games with them as my guinea pigs. My ideas would be long winded and a mess without the editing advice of Carrie and Denver. And last but not least, I need to thank my husband Jeff and kids, Sylvia and Ivan, who ate a lot of frozen foods, watched a bit too much tv and spent extra days in day care so that I could finish this book. Thank you all for your endless support.

About the Author

For more than 25 years **Mel Paradis** has performed and facilitated improv with groups ranging from preschoolers through adults. Since 2011 she has been a member of Jackson Hole, Wyoming's improv comedy troupe, The Laff Staff. In addition to improvising, Mel works as a freelance writer and Gifted and Talented teacher. Her unique background in theater, outdoor education, classroom teaching, writing and improv performance led her to create the only step by step, scope and sequence improv guide for teens on the market. Mel lives on the backside of the Teton Mountain Range in Idaho with her husband and two children.